Prayers for Generational Freedom Vol. 1

Prayers for Generational Freedom Vol. 1

Caleb Peterson

Lions of War Ministries

www.facebook.com/Lions-of-War-Ministries

Copyright © 2017 Caleb Peterson

All rights reserved.

No part of this publication may be reproduced, stored in a retrieval system, or transmitted in any form or by any means- electronic, mechanical, photocopy, recording, or any other- except for brief quotations embodied in critical articles or printed reviews, without prior permission of the publisher.

Published by Lions of War Publishing Den – A division of Lions of War Ministries.

Article {page. 1} from Dr. Paul Cox, Come up Higher {Illinois, This Joy! Books, 2010} Used by permission

Article {page. 10} Cox, Paul, Dr. "What's All This "Generational" Stuff?" Aslansplace.com. July, 15th, 2013. Used by permission

Scripture quotations marked "NKJV" are taken from the New King James Version. Copyright © 1982 Thomas Nelson, Inc. Used by permission. All rights reserved.

Scripture quotations marked "NASB" are taken from the New American Standard Bible, Copyright © 1960, 1962, 1963, 1968, 1971, 1972, 1973, 1975, 1977, 1995 by The Lockman Foundation. Used by permission.

Scripture quotations marked "NLT" are taken from the Holy Bible, New Living Translation, Copyright © 1996, 2004, 2007 by Tyndale House Foundation. Used by permission of Tyndale House Publishers, Inc. Carol Stream, Illinois 60188. All rights reserved.

Scripture quotations marked "CJB" are taken from the *Complete Jewish Bible*, Copyright © 1998 by David H. Stern. Published by Jewish New Testament Publication, Inc. www.messianicjewish.net/jntp. Distributed by Messianic Jewish Resources. Www.messianicjewish.net. All rights reserved. Used by permission.

Scripture quotations marked "AMP" or "Amplified Bible" are taken from the Amplified Bible, Copyright © 1954, 1958, 1962, 1964, 1965, 1987 by the Lockman Foundation. Used by permission. www.Lockman.org

Scripture quotations marked "AMPC" are taken from the Amplified Bible Classic Version, Copyright © 1954, 1958, 1962, 1964, 1965, 1987 by the Lockman Foundation. Used by permission. www.Lockman.org

"Scripture quotations marked ESV are from The Holy Bible, English Standard Version {ESV} copyright © 2001 by Crossway, a publishing ministry of Good News Publishers. Used by permission. All rights reserved.

Scripture quotations marked "KJV" are taken from the Holy Bible, King James Version. {Public Domain}

ISBN:0998867608
ISBN-13:9780998867601

DEDICATION TO:

First and foremost I want to thank my God, my Father, my Bridegroom for always being there in love and affection. You never gave up on me and You never will. I love You more than the air I breathe.
Secondly, to all the friends and family who never left me even during the tough times. And were there in encouragement, prayer, and support during the creation of my ministry and the production of this book. I would have never have accomplished this if it wasn't for your love, support, and encouragement. Thank you all so very much.

FROM THE AUTHOR

My heart is to help people break, shatter, and destroy everything that holds them back from coming into the full birthright and destiny God has called them to, and run the race before them as fast as they can without the weights and hindrances that attempt to slow them down. To help them break all the chains in their lives that keep them from giving themselves in reckless and total abandonment to Jesus Christ. To see them come into deeper and deeper levels of purity and freedom. And to see them come into the spiritual and physical authority God has called them to, to see them operate in the double anointing and the twofold mantle of the King and the Priest. To see them live in the amazing blissful ecstasy that can be our life in Christ.

It is my sincere hope and prayer that the prayers within this book serve as a stepping stone that helps individuals on their voyage of attaining new levels of freedom, on their journey of discovering new rooms within the heart of God, as well as the amazing adventure that leads us on roads never before trodden.

~ Caleb Peterson ~

Prayers for Generational Freedom

CONTENTS

1	Prologue 1: Why Pray Generational Prayers	1
2	Prologue 2: What's All This "Generational" Stuff	10
3	Matthew 25:31-46	18
4	Prayer to Unseat Unrighteous Hierarchy over Me and My Generational Line	22
5	Prayer to Awaken our Righteous Desires and Longings	34
6	Renunciation of Generational Idolatry	44
7	Renunciation of Generational Predatorism	51
8	Prayer to Remove One From the Dungeons of the Deep	59
9	Phantom Zone Prayer	73
10	Unrighteous Spies or Watchers Prayer	79
11	Righteous Intimacy Prayer	83
12	Prayer to Break the Curse of Unrighteous Singleness	88
13	Prayer to Break Unrighteous Networks and Setups Between Future Spouses	97
14	Prayer to Remove the Dogs of War	104
15	Unrighteous Silence and Darkness Prayer	110
16	Prayer to Break the Unrighteous Pull of the Catholic Church	115
17	Renunciation of Generational Anxiety and Worry	123
18	Renunciation of Rejecting Righteous Masculinity and Male Protection	129
19	Prayer of Repentance for Demeaning the Death,	139

Resurrection, and Blood of Jesus Christ

20	Prayer to Unseat the Unholy Female Trinity From Over Me and My Generational Line	145
21	Prayer to Remove Kali and Shiva From in Between Married Couples	165
22	Marriage Prayer	178
23	Repentance of Standing in Defiance of the Laws of God	187
24	The Truth of God	193
25	Repentance of All Selfish Love	200
26	Famine of the Truth and the Word of God	206
27	Proverbs Prayer	213
28	Rescue From Neverland	225
29	Warrior Prayer	234
30	Renunciation of all Unrighteous, Controlling, and Manipulative Words and Prayers	244

~ PROLOGUE 1 ~
WHY PRAY GENERATIONAL PRAYERS?
Dr. Paul Cox

I must admit that I have frequently asked myself, "What is so important about praying written generational prayers?" After all, at the point of placing our trust in the Lord Jesus Christ, we are saved. What more needs to be done? I am not the only one who asks this question. Over the years, many have suggested that we should not have to pray written prayers, and even that praying them is unbiblical.

Others have also questioned whether we should repent for generational issues. I have been told, sometimes in hateful ways, that this also is unbiblical and certainly not necessary. Many would say that "the work was finished at the cross of Christ and nothing else needs to be done. The matter is settled. We already have all we need. No more praying about generational issues is necessary."

Now, here is the crux of the issue. For twenty years, I have ministered to hundreds of people. Through generational praying and leading others to pray written prayers, I have seen believers transformed by the power of the Lord. This transformation has led to a deeper level of intimacy with Jesus Christ and new levels of freedom. So, how do I reconcile this apparent contradiction between the finished work of the Cross and what I have seen in ministry over the past twenty years? The Bible, not our experience, is our ultimate authority. At any point where experience and the Bible disagree, the Bible wins. I believe that and I practice that. So, what does the Bible say?

Here are the fundamentals. We are saved by grace.

Ephesians 2:8-10: For by grace you have been saved through faith, and that not of yourselves; it is the gift of God, not of works, lest anyone should boast. For we are His workmanship, created in Christ Jesus for good works, which God prepared beforehand that we should walk in them. Our works, in our Christian life, verify that we really are saved.

James 2:17-20: Thus also faith by itself, if it does not have works, is dead. But someone will say, "You have faith, and I have works." Show me your faith without your works, and I will show you my faith by my works. You believe that there is one God. You do well. Even the demons believe—and tremble! But do you want to know, O foolish man, that faith without works is dead?

Having established that we are saved by grace and our works verify our salvation, what part do we play in this process? Some argue that we have no part. It is true that salvation is the work of Christ alone. Even our coming to faith is made possible by the drawing of the Holy Spirit. The book of Romans clearly indicates that sanctification is a process; it is accomplished through the working of Christ in us, transforming us through the power of the Holy Spirit. So the question must be asked again, "Do we have any responsibility in our transformation from glory to ever-increasing glory?"

I believe the answer is yes. We do have a responsibility in our transformation from glory to ever increasing glory. Look at Philippians 2:12-13:
Therefore, my beloved, as you have always obeyed, not as in my presence only, but now much more in my absence, work out your own salvation with fear and trembling; for it is God who works in you both to will and to do for His good pleasure.

The key phrase to examine is "work out your own salvation." What does this mean? It certainly does not mean work for your salvation. Scripture is clear that salvation comes through faith and not through works. We must understand what this "working out of our salvation" means.

This issue is foundational to what I do in ministry, the reasoning behind publishing a book on prayers. If there is no scriptural mandate for this kind of ministry, then pursuing it is error. With this in mind I would like to give an extended quote from the Baker Exegetical Commentary on the New Testament. I am aware that it is a little tedious and will take some concentration on the part of the reader! However, if the importance of a believer's part in maturing, in "working out our salvation" cannot be settled, then this book is meaningless! With this in mind, here is a section from the theological discussion of Philippians 2:12.

But, the Biblical concept of salvation is not thus restricted to justification; more commonly what is in view includes God's redemptive work in its totality. Thus, while in a very important sense, we have already been saved (Eph. 2:5, 8; Titus 3:5), in another sense, we are yet to be saved (Rom. 5:9-10; 1 Cor. 3:15; 5:5; 2 Tim. 4:18). Calvin rightly claims "that salvation is taken to mean the entire course of our calling, and that this term includes all things by which God accomplishes that perfection, to which He has determined us by His free election." Because salvation in its entire scope necessarily includes the manifestation of righteousness in our lives, it follows that our activity is integral to the process of salvation; we can never afford to forget the juxtaposition between verse 9 ("not of works") and verse 10 ("for good works") in Eph. 2. In the particular context of Phil. 2, the out workings of the believer's personal salvation take the form of corporate obligations within the Christian community: the duty of seeking the good of others.

For those who admit the soteriological thrust of the passage, the tendency is to define verse 12 by means of verse

13 (or verse 13 by means of verse 12), that is, to tone down human activity by appealing to divine grace (or vice versa). One may, for example, so emphasize the truth that God does not force us to act against our will, that as a result, grace is restricted to little more than spiritual aid: "God will help us along, but it's really up to us." Conversely, fear of legalism may lead us to a more or less passive understanding of sanctification: "Our responsibility is simply to rest in God's grace, to let Him work in us." The text itself, by its very juxtaposition of those two emphases, cries out loudly against any such attempts at resolution. And the point here is not merely that both the human and the divine are stressed, but that in one and the same passage, we have what is perhaps the strongest Biblical expression of each element.

Note first Paul's concern with human activity. Although several New Testament verses place considerable emphasis on the role of human responsibility in salvation (cf. esp. 2 Pet. 1:10, "for as long as you practice these things, you will never stumble"), none puts it so bluntly as Phil. 2:12. The very choice of the verb katergazomai is notable. Chrysostom explained this compound form as indicating "with great effort, with great care"; though the evidence speaks against seeing such a nuance in the verb itself, we should not completely overlook the fact that this ancient Greek speaker perceived the term as emphatic. Bauer's "achieve, accomplish" brings us closer to the distinctive nuance of the verb; he rightly places Phil. 2:12 under the second heading, "bring about, produce, create." It is impossible to tone down the force with which Paul here points to our conscious activity in sanctification. The thought should give us pause: our salvation, which we confess to be God's from beginning to end, is here described as something that we must bring about.

For all that, our dependence on divine activity for

sanctification is nowhere made as explicit as here. To begin with, God's work is viewed as having a causal relation to our working (gajr, gar, for); our activity is possible only because of divine grace. Second, the syntax is emphatic: Paul says not merely "God works" (ho theos energei) but "the One Who works, the working is God" (theos . . . estin ho energon . . . to energein). Third, the divine influence is said to extend not only to our activity but to our very wills—a unique statement, though the idea is implied in other passages (e.g., John 1:13; Rom. 9:16). Calvin comments: "There are, in any action, two principal parts, the will, and the effective power. Both of these [Paul] ascribes to God; what more remains to us to glory in?" Fourth, the apostle reinforces our dependence on God's sovereignty with a concluding reference to "his good pleasure", a distinctly theological term used to describe divine grace.

The point is that, while sanctification requires conscious effort and concentration, our activity takes place not in a legalistic spirit, with a view to gaining God's favor, but rather in a spirit of humility and thanksgiving, recognizing that without Christ we can do nothing (cf. John 15:5), and so He alone deserves the glory.

God's working in us is not suspended because we work, nor our working suspended because God works. Neither is the relation strictly one of cooperation as if God did His part and we did ours so that the conjunction or coordination of both produced the required result. God works and we also work. But the relation is that because God works, we work. All working out of salvation on our part is the effect of God's working in us. . . . We have here not only the explanation of all acceptable activity on our part, but we also have the incentive to our willing and working. . . . The more persistently active we are in working, the more persuaded we may be that all the energizing grace and power is of God.

Let me summarize this excerpt. First, it is Christ who works in us both in salvation and in transforming us after salvation. Second, we have a part in bringing our salvation to completion. Third, our part is in the context of the church, the redeemed body of Christ.

What is stated in logical form in Philippians is illustrated in story form in the book of Joshua. The Lord clearly states that the land of Israel has been given to the children of Israel.

Moses My servant is dead. Now therefore arise, go over this Jordan, you and all this people, to the land which I am giving to them—the children of Israel. Every place that the sole of your foot will tread upon I have given to you, as I said to Moses. Joshua 1:2-3

Verse three delineates an important condition for receiving this gift. The land which has been totally given to them must be possessed by them. Joshua 1:3 says, "Every place that the sole of your foot will tread upon I have given you, as I said to Moses." The children of Israel have a part in possessing the land. They cannot simply cross over the river Jordan, set up camp, and wait for the coming of the Lord. They must possess their possessions. How do they do this? They must "walk" out their responsibility. "Every place that the soles of your feet tread, I have given to you!"

In other words, they must come against the strongholds in the land, take them down, and possess the land. This is a picture of the Christian life. We come into the Promised Land, that is, the Kingdom of God, through the blood of Christ. The word Jordan actually means "to spread judgment." As we walk through the River Jordan, judgment does not touch us because it has been held back by the power of the Lord. We enter into the land and begin to take down, through the power of God, the strongholds in our lives. God does His part and we do our part. Our part includes the use of spiritual disciplines as well as being intentional about getting all the deliverance from the old nature that we can. That is where generational prayers come in.

I understand from personal experience that those who do not believe in generational deliverance or in praying written generational prayers will not be satisfied by any reasoning or evidence. After I had been ministering deliverance for several months as a Baptist pastor, several of the deacons came to me to express their concerns. Some of our discussions became very intense! Finally, one deacon said to me, "Well, if this is really true, then where is the fruit?" The point was well taken. To show him the fruit, I scheduled a Sunday evening service where several people who had been significantly helped by prayers for generational deliverance gave testimonies of what the Lord had done. The evening was very powerful. For over two hours, person after person came to the microphone and shared how the Lord had touched their lives. The testimonies were particularly meaningful because I had ministered to some of these people for nine years before I started doing deliverances.

Clearly it was the ministry of deliverance that had made a difference! After the service, that same deacon came to me and said, "I do not care what all those people say, I do not believe in this ministry." At the following deacon meeting, the debate continued. Finally, in frustration, I said to the board, "If you do not want me to help these people, then you help them!" I was shocked by their response. They all raised their hands and said, "We can't." Here was the real heart of the issue. Those who do not believe in this ministry not only do not believe in it, but they also have no answers or alternative solutions to offer believers who continue to be in pain. Their only answer is their own personal Biblical and theological response to the concept of praying for people.

All of this should not be a surprise to anyone who

knows the Bible. Jesus also encountered religious people who came against His healing and deliverance ministry. One of the most shocking scriptures in the Bible is the account of the raising of Lazarus from the dead.

Now when He had said these things, He cried with a loud voice, "Lazarus, come forth!" And he who had died came out bound hand and foot with grave clothes, and his face was wrapped with a cloth. Jesus said to them, "Loose him, and let him go." Then many of the Jews who had come to Mary, and had seen the things Jesus did, believed in Him. But some of them went away to the Pharisees and told them the things Jesus did. Then the chief priests and the Pharisees gathered a council and said, "What shall we do? For this Man works many signs. If we let Him alone like this, everyone will believe in Him, and the Romans will come and take away both our place and nation." And one of them, Caiaphas, being high priest that year, said to them, "You know nothing at all, nor do you consider that it is expedient for us that one man should die for the people, and not that the whole nation should perish." Now this he did not say on his own authority; but being high priest that year he prophesied that Jesus would die for the nation, and not for that nation only, but also that He would gather together in one the children of God who were scattered abroad. Then, from that day on, they plotted to put Him to death.

What is so shocking? Here is Jesus raising someone from the dead. Think of the joy of Lazarus and the joy of those who loved him; but, the religious people do not see this. All they can see are their own agendas and beliefs. Truth is not the issue! Their only response to the raising of Lazarus from the dead was to plot Jesus' death.

The deacon meetings at my Baptist church finally culminated in congregational meetings. The debate seemed endless! Finally, I decided I had to leave the church. I can remember a conversation right after the meeting. I turned to a friend and said, "All I have ever wanted to do in ministry is to help others. Now, that I am finally able to really help people, the deacons won't let me." I walked away crushed. But the Lord was not finished with me or with the ministry of deliverance. His heart is to see His people set free. In obedience, I have followed His calling on my life. Years later, the fruit is evident. The Lord has been faithful. Yes, there is resistance, but lives are being changed.

~ PROLOGUE 2 ~
WHAT'S ALL THIS "GENERATIONAL" STUFF?

Dr. Paul Cox

Exodus 20:5 *You shall not bow down yourself to them or serve them [idols]; for I the Lord your God am a jealous God, visiting the iniquity of the fathers upon the children to the third and fourth generation of those who hate Me, But showing mercy and steadfast love to a thousand generations of those who love Me and keep My commandments.*

We believe the issue of generational iniquity is best illustrated in the familiar story of Cain. Let's review. Cain and his brother Abel brought a sacrifice to the Lord; Abel's sacrifice was found worthy in God's eyes, while Cain's was not. This story marks an important distinction between sin, rebellion and iniquity. When Cain became angry, sad and dejected, the Lord said to Cain, "Sin crouches at your door; its desire is for you, but you must master it." In response to this, Cain did three things. First, and perhaps most profoundly, he departed from the presence of the Lord. Next, he convinced his brother to come out to the fields, where he killed him. Lastly, when the Lord asked him where his brother was, Cain replied, "Am I my brother's keeper?" And after this answer, the Lord cursed Cain.

We may define sin simply as separation from God, and Cain's "departing from the presence of the Lord" exemplifies this. In the Old Testament, the law required sin offerings for such things as coming in contact with a dead animal carcass or a dead body, so we can see that sin occurs from actions as simple as taking our eyes off God and going astray; there is not necessarily any malicious intent. Rebellion, on the other hand, occurs when we knowingly do that which God has commanded us and charged us not to do, when we "do it anyway."

For generational issues, however, iniquity becomes our primary concern, and Cain's answer to God exemplifies iniquity. The Lord asks Cain, "Where is your brother?" and Cain does not say, "Lord, I have sinned greatly, for I have committed murder upon my own brother." He does not even respond rebelliously, "Listen, I know it's against the rules, but I killed Abel, so could we just get this punishment thing over with, Lord?" Instead, he replies, "Am I my brother's keeper?" Cain gives an answer that distorts the truth; he chooses not to confess the truth with contrition, nor to tell the truth, albeit without remorse (like the second example response), but his response is crafted to cover his sin and rebellion, and thus evade consequences altogether.

Thus, we may define iniquity as a twisted response to God. The Hebrew word avown is translated here as iniquity, and this word comes from the root word avah, which Strong's translates as "do amiss, bow down, make crooked, pervert." God curses Cain for his actions, and Cain replies, "My punishment is too great!" The word translated as "punishment" is actually avown; so Cain is quite literally saying, "My crookedness is too great," where 'crookedness' may refer to either his own crooked ways, the punishment that comes with them, or both. Thus, it is quite literally this crookedness, this twisting of the father's that is visited upon the sons in the sense of the curse, the punishment, but also in the sense of the distorted response.

Let's get some perspective. The Father sent His Son Jesus to atone once and for all for our sins on the cross. He bore the weight of all our sins, and He became a curse for us, so that we might have freedom. He has conquered sin once and for all. He alone could bear it. The victory is His. If we can become as Paul described, so that "it is not me who lives, but Christ in me," then we can carry His victory in us. We believe the Father "visits the iniquity of the fathers on the sons" not because He has a heart to burden people, but so that they may be confronted with this twisting of the truth, rise to the challenge and overcome it, not through our own righteousness, but through the righteous sacrifice of the One Who lives in us (that is, Jesus). We believe this occurs so that the sons may be presented with this wrong response, perceive this sin, and be given the opportunity to "master it" that their fathers squandered. Rev 3:5 says the following:

Thus shall he who conquers be clad in white garments, and I will not erase or blot out his name from the Book of Life; I will acknowledge him as Mine, and I will confess his name openly before My Father and before His angels. The reward is promised to be great for those who persevere and learn to overcome.

That's So Old Testament!
Yes. That is exactly where it is.

Consider this question: What is a Testament? The American Heritage Dictionary defines it this way: Something that serves as tangible proof or evidence. It comes from the Latin word testis, which can be translated roughly to mean "witness." Who or what does the Old Testament give evidence of? Who or What is it a witness to? You're probably already rolling your eyes, because of course it is God that the Old Testament gives witness to. But don't shrug this aside; it's the reason we still carry all those pages around in our Bibles. The testament may be old, but as for the God it testifies of, HE IS still the same. He does not change. If doubt still lingers about the relevance of the Old Testament, consider Luke 16:31, wherein Jesus gave us some stunning words in His parable about the rich man and the beggar,

Lazarus:

But Abraham said, "If they won't listen to Moses and the prophets, they won't listen even if someone rises from the dead."

Those are probably not particularly comforting words. Those who find themselves echoing the objection about generational iniquity being confined to the Old Testament probably consider Gal 5:3-4, which says this:

If you are trying to find favor with God by being circumcised, you must obey all of the regulations in the whole law of Moses. For if you are trying to make yourselves right with God by keeping the law, you have been cut off from Christ! You have fallen away from God's grace.

Much of the Old Testament (though not all by any means) describes God's commands to the Israelites, in other words, the law. Paul exhorts us here not to try and work out our salvation through the law. But even in the Old Testament, God expresses contempt for songs, offerings and festivals because of the people's attitude. All of these were in keeping with the law. The Lord almost killed Balaam for having a wrong attitude and being spiritually insensitive, even though he was following the command of the Lord.

The law was created to give witness to God, to His holiness. It was created to guard us from sin before we put faith in Jesus (Gal 3:24). It was also created to produce guilt in us, which would, in turn, reveal to us our inability to produce right standing with God through our own efforts (Gal 3:19). For that, we need a Savior. Jesus lived his life in perfect submission to the law, so that we would not place our faith in the law, but in the One who fulfilled it. Again, He said, "I came not to abolish the law, but to fulfill it." Through Him, we can live in harmony as Paul describes in Eph 2:20:

*We are His house, built on the foundation of the **apostles** and the **prophets**. And the cornerstone is Christ Jesus Himself.* (Bold added for emphasis)

God can change and has changed His commands in keeping with His time or season. Acts 11 describes how He repealed the commands to only eat the flesh of certain animals just before the first Gentiles received the Spirit. In the verse above, Paul fervently urges the brethren against circumcision. To use an exaggerated example, we would certainly strain ourselves if we tried to simultaneously worship the Lord with joyous shouts and clapping, mourn with loud crying and moaning, and receive Him in quietness and rest.

But the part of Exodus 20:5 describing generational iniquity has no command. It's not the law. It is not even an impersonal, categorical description of how God's legal system works, such as, "The wages of sin are death." Exodus 20:5 describes God! Read it again:

...for I the Lord your God am a jealous God, visiting the iniquity of the fathers upon the children to the third and fourth generation of those who hate Me, But showing mercy and steadfast love to a thousand generations of those who love Me and keep My commandments.

This describes not the law, but a characteristic of God's ways and His justice. The Lord loves righteousness right now just as much as He did in the days of Adam. He still does not despise those with a contrite heart and a broken spirit. And although He sent Jesus to be a friend to sinners and release us from its bondage, He still hates sin. What He tells us to do may depend on context, but His character does not change.

Lest there be any confusion about the subject of generational sin in our New Covenant times, consider the words of the Lord in Luke 11:47-51 (Amplified):

Woe to you! For you are rebuilding and repairing the tombs of the prophets, whom your fathers killed. So you bear witness and give your full approval and consent to the deeds of your fathers; for they actually killed them, and you rebuild and repair monuments *to them...**So that the blood of all the prophets shed from the foundation of the world may be charged against and required of this age and generation.*** (Bold added for emphasis)

Clearly, Jesus is explicitly telling us here that as these sons faced the sins of their fathers, they could be held accountable for them according to the way they responded. The Pharisees chose to honor the prophets in much the same way that they honored Jesus; they honored Him with their mouths, but their hearts were far from Him. The word hypocrisy comes from the word for "actor," or "play-acting." The honor of the Pharisees was an act. They performed this act so that they would be seen honoring Jesus and the prophets; they were courting the favor of the people and seeking to be esteemed by those who loved Jesus and the prophets. They loved the honor of men, and they loved for men to bow down to them in public.

Deep generational iniquity was being passed down from their fathers, and they chose to treat the outside; they were coating that sin and sealing it in with a thick lacquer of whitewash. I know the following sounds cheeky, but rather, I mean it quite literally and sincerely: if you have issues with a generational paradigm, please take them up with the Lord. Romans 14:23 tells us that whatever does not originate and proceed from faith is sin, so until the day arrives when the Lord allows you to accept a generational paradigm on faith, we will have to live in patience according to Romans 14:3:
The man who eats everything must not look down on him who does not, and the man who does not eat everything must not condemn the man who does, for God has accepted him.

Until that day, we'll just have to believe in a great God, Who is above and beyond all the ways of men, and accepts all kinds of people just for having faith in Jesus Christ.

Okay, I get the idea, but...so what?

So we know that iniquity can be passed down through

the generations (thus the term, "generational iniquity"), and we have a very vague idea of what it looks like. We can conceive a seemingly infinite number of scenarios that might indicate the presence of generational iniquity. Generally, though, we look for patterns of destruction and devouring that occur pervasively and repeatedly throughout a family. From here, we do something which we call, "identificational repentance," a big term that simply means we:

1.) perceive, through the Spirit, the presence of the twistedness, the iniquity,
2.) identify with those in our family line who fell into this sin (as in Dan 9),
3.) confess it as sin,
4.) place that sin in the hands of Jesus on the cross, and
5.) turn away from it and turn back to God (repent).

We also ask the Lord to remove the curses and consequences that resulted from that iniquity. In other words, the process is the same process of repentance described repeatedly by the prophets, and for that matter, by Jesus. The only wrinkle unique to identificational repentance is that we intentionally choose to identify with those in our family line, rather than being like the Pharisee who says, "Thank you, God, that you didn't make me like that sinner." God expresses His heart for this repentance clearly in Leviticus 26:40:

But at last, my people will confess their sins and the sins of their ancestors for betraying me and being hostile toward me.

In this way, we can "work out our salvation through fear and trembling."

We must be careful, however, as we walk through this process, to rely on the guidance of the Holy Spirit, for we cannot conquer iniquity through our own power or might, but only by His Spirit, Who is released to us through our faith in Jesus. I write this as an aside, but please, let my words implore you to understand this as the primary and the most important caveat of all. Do what you must to get this imprinted; picture a drill sergeant; imagine the sound of thunder booming through these words as you reread them:

Rely on the Holy Spirit

So, long story short: identify with those who committed the sin, and repent, through the leadership of the Holy Spirit. I emphasize this again because we cannot manipulate God. He is indeed Jehovah Raphe. He is indeed healing. He is the liberation we seek. But we cannot force His hand by our actions, our formulas, our procedures, or our protocols into acting in a particular manner. He does it because He wants to, because He is our Father and He loves us so much He sent Jesus to bear all the weight that we cannot. He does not act because we found the secret formula to force His hand, or because of our own merits, but because of Who He Is.

MATTHEW 25:31-46
Caleb Peterson

One night I was praying and fellowshipping with the Holy Spirit. Seeking Him and asking Him to show me areas in my life that I needed healing and cleansing, something I do fairly often for one of my main goals in life is to live out two of my favorite verses.

Psalms 19:14
14 Let the words of my mouth and the meditation of my heart
Be acceptable and pleasing in Your sight,
Oh Lord, my {firm, immovable} rock and my Redeemer.
~ Amplified Bible ~
Proverbs 22:11
11 He who loves purity of heart
And has grace on his lips,
The King will be his friend. **~ NKJV ~**

I try to regularly seek God in order to grow into deeper and deeper levels of purity and freedom in all aspects of my life.
So as I was praying I heard the phrase "Everlasting punishment". This phrase surprised me, I had never heard of an everlasting punishment before. I had never heard of a punishment that was never ending. So I continued to pray into it, and as I did I saw something over me and my generational line. It looked to be dark chains of some sort. So naturally, I wanted them dealt with. I started searching scripture fervently. Then after a while, I found it. I discovered it in the book of Matthew. After reading through these verses I knew this was something I needed to repent of on behalf of myself and my generational line. I sure didn't want an everlasting punishment to keep me from reaching

every place God had ordained for me to experience.

I felt like the Holy Spirit was prodding me to write a prayer about this. At first, I felt it would be very complicated to do so, and that it would take a lot of study in order to write a prayer. In that moment it seemed like the Holy Spirit slapped me in the back of the head. Like a Gibbs slap, for those of you who have seen NCIS. He brought back to my memory something my Dad had once told me. He told me that sometimes the shortest and simplest prayers were the most powerful. So I sat down and asked the Holy Spirit to come and guide me as I wrote the prayer. I opened my Bible and just wrote the prayer as simply as I could. After I was done I prayed through the prayer and I could feel something lifting. I do believe it was the everlasting punishment that was put upon my generational line because of our sins. This is a short simple prayer, but I believe it is very powerful.

Caleb Peterson

~ PRAYER ~
MATTHEW 25:31-46

I repent and renounce on behalf of myself and my generational line for all those who came against and attacked the weak and helpless, instead of defending and protecting them.

I repent and renounce for all those who starved and deprived the famished and the hungry, instead of feeding them.

I repent and renounce for all those who denied the thirsty and the parched drink; instead of sharing the wealth of their wells.

I repent and renounce for all those who ignored and dismissed the naked, instead of clothing them.

I repent and renounce for all those who neglected and forgot about those in prison, instead of attending to and visiting them.

Lord, we come before Your Holy Throne, kneeling in reverence and repentance.
We ask for Your forgiveness. For when we did these things when we turned the least of these away, we turned You away. And in doing so we reaped upon ourselves an everlasting punishment.
Lord, forgive us for any time we rejected You in any form or rejected any aspect of You and Your divine nature.

Lord, as a member of this generational line I repent and I ask that You would remove the everlasting punishment that was put upon us because of our sins.

Lord, please lift this punishment from me and my generational line as we repent and cry out for forgiveness and mercy.

Lord, I ask that it would be replaced with an everlasting blessing.

We throw ourselves on the mercy of the court. Please forgive us, and cleanse us spirit, soul, and body from any and all defilement that came upon us from this everlasting punishment.

Caleb Peterson

PRAYER TO UNSEAT UNRIGHTEOUS HIERARCHY OVER ME AND MY GENERATIONAL LINE
Caleb Peterson

This prayer was kinda birthed out of necessity. A friend of mine was having a few problems. The main one was seizures that the doctors couldn't really explain. They couldn't seem to figure out what was going on, why he was having these seizures. So he came to me for help. Thankfully he gave me a few weeks head notice, so I could prepare. I started praying into it asking God what would cause this to come over him. I started to feel like something big and nasty had been allowed to come over him and his generational line. What it was I didn't know just yet.

I started seeking God and asking for clues as to what this unrighteous being was and how it got there. My gut told me it had to do with someone stepping out in authority they didn't have, and praying over a city or a state attacking the principalities over a region. I started to slowly write a prayer as I prayed through it all, and of course sought discernment help from friends I knew and trusted. I went to one of my best friends who had interned with Dr. Paul Cox as well. I asked him if he discerned anything. He discerned pretty much the same thing I did. He sensed that someone had come against an unrighteous being that they were not supposed to.

I know this might sound strange, but this is actually pretty common in Christians circles. Whether it's on a prayer walk or praying over their city or state, Christians assume that because they are Christians that they can pray against any unrighteous being they come against. Or they don't realize the spiritual aspect of certain things they are praying against and so they don't realize they are stirring up a hornet's nest. There are unrighteous beings that God has called us to wage war against and so he gave us the authority to do so. And then there are unrighteous beings, that only God himself can rebuke and deal with. There are beings over cities, states, and countries; {such as unrighteous hierarchy}, that are strong enough only God Himself can deal with them. We even see this in scripture.

Jude 1:8-9
8 Nevertheless in the same way, these dreamers {who are dreaming that God will not punish them} also defile the body, and reject {legitimate} authority, and revile and mock angelic majesties.
9 But even the archangel Michael, when he was disputing with the devil {Satan}, and arguing about the body of Moses, did not dare bring an abusive condemnation against him, but {simply} said, "The Lord rebuke you!" ~ **Amplified Bible** ~

So we see that even Michael the Archangel, one of the strongest, toughest, and mightiest warrior in this vast cosmos, even he wouldn't bring a slanderous word against Lucifer. He said, "The Lord rebuke you." He didn't attempt to take on Lucifer himself because he knew his place and he knew where his sphere of authority began and ended. There are unrighteous beings in this universe that we cannot and shouldn't even attempt to take on. For we don't have the authority to do so, and therefore all we manage to do is put a target on our back. It's like going into the forest and seeking out the biggest grizzly bear we can find and then poking him with a sharp stick. It's not only stupid, it's dangerous! Michael the archangel is one of these most dangerous and violent warriors in this vast cosmos, and even he didn't come against certain unrighteous beings. Because he knew where his authority ended, and that only

God had the power and authority to deal with some of them. We need to take this example to heart and be very careful not to take on anything or any being that God hasn't directly instructed us to. If God hasn't instructed us to take it on, then we do not have the authority to do so.

So, whether it was my client or his generational line someone had attacked or come against an unrighteous being whether it was over a city or state I don't know. But they came against this being through prayer, which only succeeded in making the being mad and opened the door allowing it to attack and harass them. I believe that this dynamic was what was causing these seizures. So, I started writing the prayer and as I did my friend and I discerned and heard more as we went on. This prayer is the result. During the session with my client, I had him pray through this prayer as well as other prayers. After the session, his seizures left and didn't come back. Thank you, God! I believe this prayer had something to do with that victory, but of course, I can't prove that. But I do hope and pray that this prayer touches you all and helps you rid your life of the junk that has come upon you through your sins and the sins of your ancestors.

~ PRAYER ~
PRAYER TO UNSEAT UNRIGHTEOUS HIERARCHY OVER ME AND MY GENERATIONAL LINE

I renounce and repent for all those in my generational line who were audacious and arrogant and came against, attacked, and slandered any unrighteous spiritual beings. Especially for all those who because of arrogance or ignorance came against, attacked, or slandered any unrighteous celestial beings, unrighteous cosmic beings, or any other unrighteous hierarchy; instead of letting the Lord deal with them. Which in turn allowed these unrighteous beings to come against and take a high place of authority over me and my generational line.

I repent and renounce for all those who defiled their physically and spiritually bodies by rejecting any and all forms of authority.
I repent and renounce for all those who reviled and mocked angelic majesties, believing that God would not bring justice and judgment upon them for these sins.

I repent for all those in my generational line who consumed and engorged themselves on the corrupt passions of the sinful nature of this world.
I repent for all those who hated, mocked, reviled, or despised authority in any form.
I repent for all those who were reckless, presumptuous, ignorant, arrogant, and would only be ruled by their own

will. And were foolish and operated in unrighteous boldness and did not tremble with they mocked or reviled angelic majesties. ~ 1 ~

I repent on behalf of myself and my generational line for all those who dedicated future generations to Satan, any unrighteous hierarchy, or any other unrighteous spiritual beings.
Lord, please break the consequences of these sins off of me and my generational line.

I repent for all those in my generational line who offered up unrighteous worship or performed any rituals of worship to any unrighteous hierarchy, worshiping them as gods.
I repent for all those who performed any rituals of worship, dedications, or sacrifices on any unrighteous altar.
I repent for all those who sacrificed children, blood, DNA, body parts, or organs to any unrighteous hierarchy.

I repent for all those who danced before, who committed sexual acts, and who burnt offerings in any rituals to any pagan deities or any other unrighteous being.
I repent for all those who participated in unrighteous intercession, who performed unholy communions, who communed with the dead, and who joined in as well as participating in rituals, dedications, or sacrifices with unrighteous priests and priestesses.
Lord, please break, shatter, cut off, and destroy any unrighteous ties, cords, ropes, chains, shackles, and bindings that have been allowed to tie me and my generational line to any unrighteous altar, because of my sins or the sins of my ancestors.

I repent for all those who dedicated or gave away pieces of land that God had given them; to evil men, Satan, or any other unrighteous spiritual beings, thus defiling and cursing the land that God had given them to guard and steward.

I repent for all those in my generational line who worshiped the land that God had given them, rather than worshiping the Creator who created and formed the land.

I repent for all those who performed any type of ritual of worship of the land on our around a righteous or unrighteous altar.

I repent for all those who performed ritual sacrifices with dirt, plants, or anything pertaining to the land, on righteous or unrighteous altars.

I repent for all those who either participated in or sat back and watched, allowing these sins to be committed on the land that God had given them.

Lord, please break the consequences of these sins off of me and my generational line.

Lord, I ask that You would break off of me and my generational line any and all unrighteous ties or connections between us and the land.

Lord, please come with Your blood and cleanse the land that I or my ancestors defiled with sin and wickedness.

Lord, forgive us for not rightly stewarding the land that You had given us, and for defiling it instead of using it the way You intended.

Lord, I renounce and I repent for all private and communal worship of any pagan deities in my generational line.

Lord, I ask that You would disconnect me from the unrighteous table of the fellowship of pagan deities.

Lord, please remove any and all ties or connections between us and this table.

Lord, I ask that You would break any connection between me, my generational line and any pagan deities, any demonic power, or between us and any unrighteous spiritual being, that have come upon us through the evil we committed.

I repent for all those in my generational in who fellowshipped with demons, instead of fellowshipping with Jesus Christ and His Holy Spirit.

I repent for all those in my generational line who partook of the table of demons, instead of partaking of the Lord's table, and for all those who drank from the cup of demons, instead of drinking from the Lord's cup.

Lord, I now declare that my generational line and I will only fellowship with the Holy Trinity, and that we will only partake of Your table, and that we will only drink from Your cup. ~ 2 ~

Lord, I renounce and repent on behalf of myself and my generational line for all those who created and built unrighteous altars, carved images, or idols within the Temple of the Lord.

I repent for all those who built unrighteous altars to the Baals and all the starry hosts.

I repent for all those who performed any rituals of witchcraft, sorcery, wizardry, black magic, voodoo, or any other occultic ritual on any altar within the Lord's Temple. Especially for all those who performed these acts on a righteous altar, or a righteous piece of land for the sole purpose of defiling and contaminating that which is holy.

I repent for all those who performed any unrighteous rituals of dedication or performed any ritual sacrifice within the Lord's Temple.

I repent for all those who performed any unrighteous worship rituals or worshiped and praised any unrighteous hierarchy, any pagan deities, or any other unrighteous spiritual being within the Temple of the Lord.

I repent for all those who defiled a holy altar by committing unrighteous acts on or around it.

I repent for all unrighteous rituals of worship, sacrifice, all sexual acts, unrighteous intercession, unholy communions, all communing with the dead, all rituals with unrighteous music, and any other unrighteous rituals performed on a holy altar.

Lord, on behalf of myself and my generational line I repent and I ask Your forgiveness for any time we defiled Your holy places.

Lord, please break all unrighteous ties and connections between me and the altars these sins were committed on, as well as between the people that committed these sins.

Lord, please cleanse me and my generational line from all defilement that came upon us through performing or participating in these sins, wash us; spirit, soul, and body in Your blood.

I repent for all those who through evil practices entered the second heaven for any unrighteous purpose.

Lord, please break all unrighteous ties, cords, ropes, and roots between me and the second heaven that have been empowered due to any evil that I or my ancestors committed.

Lord, I ask that You would bring back to me any part of me or my generational line that is trapped in the second heaven, that was stolen or given away through our wickedness.

Lord, please remove from my generational line and myself anything from the second heaven that the enemy was allowed to plant within us. ~ 3 ~

Lord, please cleanse all parts of me that You are returning unto me.

I repent for all those who came into unrighteous union with any pagan deities, any unrighteous hierarchy, or any other unrighteous spiritual beings.

Lord, please cleanse me and my generational lines blood and

DNA from all contamination that came through these unrighteous unions.

Lord, please break all unrighteous ties and connections of any kind between my generational line and I, and any unrighteous spiritual celestial beings, unrighteous cosmic beings, any pagan deities, any unrighteous hierarchy, any other unrighteous spiritual beings, or any human being that has attempted or succeeded in taking a position of unrighteous authority over us.

In the Name of the Lord Jesus Christ, I now break all dedications of me and my generational line to any unrighteous hierarchy, any pagan deities, or any other unrighteous spiritual beings.

Lord, please come and unseat and remove all unrighteous spiritual authorities, unrighteous celestial beings, unrighteous cosmic beings, any unrighteous hierarchy, any pagan deities, and any other unrighteous spiritual beings that have been allowed to come over us, because of our ignorance, arrogance, or sins we committed.

I now command all evil associated with the above to leave me now, in the Name of the Lord Jesus Christ.

I now declare that my generational line and I belong to the Holy Godhead and to them alone.

Oh, Lion of Judah, who sits enthroned in power, might, and glory, I invite and ask You to come over me and my generational line.

I invite You to come and be the Head and the Highest Authority over me and my generational line.

I ask that You would come and overshadow us with Your power and glory, with Your strength and Your might, come and overshadow us with Your very being.

I decree and declare that as for me and my house, we will

serve the one true God forever and ever. ~ 4 ~

1. ~ ~
2 Peter 2:10-11
10 and especially those who indulge in the corrupt passions of the sin nature, and despise authority. Presumptuous and reckless, self-willed and arrogant {creatures, despising the majesty of the Lord}, they do not tremble when they revile angelic majesties,
11 whereas even angels who are superior in might and power do not bring a reviling {defaming} accusation against them before the Lord.
~ Amplified Bible ~

2. ~ ~
Paul taught that a believer would actually be joined with demonic powers if he/she became involved in the table of the fellowship of pagan deities.
1 Corinthians 10:20-22
20 Rather, that the things which the Gentiles sacrifice they sacrifice to demons and not to God, and I do not want you to have fellowship with demons.
21 You cannot drink the cup of the Lord and the cup of demons; you cannot partake of the Lord's table and of the table demons.
22 Or do we provoke the Lord to jealousy? Are we stronger than He?
~ NKJV ~
We cannot drink from the cup of the Lord and the cup of demons; we cannot partake of the Lord's table and the table of demons.
We cannot drink the wine of the Lord if we are already drinking the wine of demons. We cannot feast from the Lord's table and all that it offers, if we are eating and devouring the food of demons. Therefore we must be extremely careful who's wine we are drinking and who's table we are feasting at.

3. ~ ~
Now, of course, the second heaven is never referred to in scripture but scripture does speak of the possibility of multiple heavens.
Hebrews 4:14
14 Inasmuch then as we {believers} have a great High Priest who has {already ascended and} passed through the heavens, Jesus the Son of God, let us hold fast our confession {of faith and cling tenaciously to our absolute trust in Him as Savior}. **~ Amplified Bible ~**
The fact that it tells us that Jesus passed through the heavens, {plural} gives us fairly good evidence that there is more than one heaven out there.

Hebrews 4:14
14 Therefore, since we have a great cohen gadol who has passed through to the highest heaven, Yeshua, the Son of God, let us hold firmly to what we acknowledge as true. ~ **CJB** ~
The Complete Jewish Bible even tells us Jesus passed through to the highest heaven. Which of course would suggest there is more than one. Then, of course, the Bible talks about the third heaven.

2 Corinthians 12:2
2 I know a man in Christ who fourteen years ago—whether in the body I do not know, or whether out of the body I do not know, God knows—such a one was caught up to the third heaven. ~ **NKJV** ~
So if there is a third heaven, it would only seem natural that there would be a first and second as well. But of course, scripture does not mention them.

What we believe is that since scripture mentions the third heaven that there is indeed a first and second. The first being the atmosphere that surrounds our earthly realm. The stratosphere so to speak. Now scripture does refer to this as heaven in scripture.

Genesis 6:7
7 So the Lord said, "I will blot out man whom I have created from the face of the land, man and animals and creeping things and the birds of the heavens, for I am sorry that I have made them." ~ **ESV** ~
Now, most versions of this verse use the phrases "Birds of the air," or "Birds of the sky". Now if you look it up in the Strong's you will see that the word "air" or "sky" is translated shamayim which means heaven. It comes from the root word meaning to be lofty and high up. So our space or stratosphere would seem to be the first heaven.

Now the second heaven would be outer space, which includes the sun, the moon, the stars and all the planets.

Deuteronomy 4:19
19 And beware that you do not raise your eyes towards the heaven and see the sun and the moon and the stars, all the host of heaven, and let yourselves be led astray and worship them and serve them, {mere created bodies} which the Lord your God has allotted to {serve and benefit} all the peoples under the whole heaven. ~ **Amplified Bible** ~
In scripture, we see outer space called heaven. This would seem to apply that this is the second heaven.

Matthew 24:29
29 "Immediately after the tribulation of those days the sun will be darkened, and the moon will not give its light, and the stars will fall from heaven, and the powers of the heavens will be shaken. ~ **ESV** ~
So this would seem to say there are three heavens. The first is our

stratosphere, the air, and sky. The second outer space and all that it contains. And of course the Third heaven, God's very abode. We believe that the second heaven is the abode of the enemy. A place of very high-ranking spiritual beings in the enemies ranks.

And we must be extremely careful when praying against certain beings. Especially those connected with the second heaven. And unless God Himself directly authorizes us to engage in this kind of high-level warfare, I urge you to stay completely away. For if we attempt to step into this battle arena without God's direct say so and His protection we are opening ourselves and our generational line to major attacks from high ranking unrighteous spiritual beings. As well as parts of our spirit, soul, heart, mind, will, or emotions being imprisoned there.

4. ~ ~

Joshua 24:15

15 And if it seems evil to you to serve the Lord, choose for yourselves this day whom you will serve, whether the gods which your fathers served that were on the other side of the River, or the gods of the Amorites, in whose land you dwell. But as for me and my house, we will serve the Lord. ~ **NKJV** ~

PRAYER TO AWAKEN OUR RIGHTEOUS DESIRES AND LONGINGS
Caleb Peterson

This prayer came after a particularly rough patch of my life. Dreams had been dashed, hopes had been decimated and disappointment seemed to be around every corner. My heart was sick and hurting. After experiencing year after year of hope unfulfilled, I began to shut my heart down. I fell into despair and lost all hope. And at the time I did not realize this, but I soon would.

The Lord began leading me on a journey of not only opening my eyes to what was going on but a journey of love and healing. The first step of this journey started with a book written by one of my heroes; The Journey of Desire by John Eldredge. This book helped me to see the ways I had shut down my heart, as well as my hopes, dreams, and desires because I did not want to feel the pain anymore. I did not want to live with the agony of constant disappointment. So I had shut my heart down. I realized that as hard as it would be I needed to open my heart back up and keep my hope alive no matter how many times disappointment reared its ugly head.

Now even after all these years, He is still teaching me more and more, and I'm the first to admit I still have much more to learn. Though He continues to teach me not only through my own life but through the life of those around me.

One day after watching a friend of mine go through a rough patch, I saw her begin to completely shut her heart down to where she couldn't feel any emotion. This was more than likely a defense mechanism in order to protect the heart from further pain. But as I watched this play out in her life the Holy Spirit taught me a very valuable lesson. He showed me something I had never thought about before. If our hearts are shut down, yes, of course, we don't feel any pain. But we also can't feel love, affection, joy, etc....

When we are in pain from heartache, hope deferred, or wounds from our past; our first instinct is to shut down our hearts. No one likes to feel or experience pain and heartache. But we can't take the easy way out. No matter how painful it is. How can we get healed up if we shut our hearts down? Yes, when we shut down our hearts down we can't feel heartache or pain, but when we do this we shut out everything else as well. We shut out joy, love, affection, etc..... And when we shut these emotions out we shut out healing, as well as shutting out God Himself.

Yes, living with hope means you're going to experience heartache, pain, and the agony of a sick heart. But if we don't continually open up our hearts then we will never ever experience the amazing joy of desire fulfilled. Scripture tells us that desire fulfilled is a tree of life, growing and blossoming in our life. But we cannot experience this wonderful tree of life growing in our life if we don't open up our hearts. For we cannot desire and long for anything if our hearts are completely shut down. And if we cannot desire or long for anything, then we certainly will never come into desire fulfilled. To experience that tree of life, to experience desire fulfilled means we have to be vulnerable, and yes that means we will get hurt. Yes, that means we will encounter disappointment, but without that risk, we can never experience and receive the amazing reward of desire fulfilled. We will never truly experience the amazing bliss that comes when true love overwhelms our hearts, if we have shut our hearts down, or killed off our desires, longings, and dreams.

Many of us have killed off the dreams, desires, longings, and hopes within ourselves. And we need to repent for doing so, as well as asking God to change our mindsets. And ask Him to bring these hopes, dreams, and desires back to life. That is what was on my heart when I crafted this prayer. I hope that it blesses you as much as it has me.

~ PRAYER ~
PRAYER TO AWAKEN OUR RIGHTEOUS DESIRES AND LONGINGS

On behalf of myself and my generational line, I repent for all those who rejected, buried, or killed any of the passions, dreams, desires, or hopes that God placed within them.

I repent for not listening to the righteous passions, yearnings, and desires that God implanted within us.

On behalf of myself and my generational line, I repent for those who because others told them that they were impossible, or because they had tried and failed; they buried or killed the dreams and desires that God placed into them.

On behalf of myself and my generational line, I repent for not listening to our hearts, our desires, and our divine discontentment, but instead, we listened to our hurt, our pain, and the wounds of our past. Allowing them to dictate our actions and guide us in the way we should go.

I repent for allowing pain and heartache to dictate our actions, especially for when we allowed them to cause us to shut down our hearts completely. Yes, we couldn't feel the heartache and pain, but with our hearts shut down we couldn't feel love or affection either. And therefore, our hearts remained wounded and scarred.

I repent and renounce on behalf of myself and my generational line for giving up, losing heart, and for camping in places of resignation and indulgence, for in doing so we allowed ourselves to be trapped in prisons of hopelessness, depression, and despair.

On behalf of myself and my generational line, I repent for refusing to love because we had been hurt, and for forsaking our dreams because our hopes had been deferred. And therefore our hearts became sick, and instead of crying out to God to heal our wounded sick hearts and allow Him to open them up to love again, we shut down our hearts altogether. ~ 1 ~

I repent on behalf of myself and my generational for any time that we clung to false hope, instead of seeking after and holding on tight to true hope that only comes from God above.

Lord, on behalf of myself and my generational line I repent for listening to others who said that desire was evil and told us to kill it and call it sanctification.

I repent for the sin of shutting our hearts down, for when we did this we not only couldn't feel Your love towards us, but we also killed the desires and passions that You Lord had put into us. Therefore, in fact, we told You that You didn't know what You were doing, and we murdered part of the very essence of God that He had put into our beings.

I repent for allowing the enemy and other people to convince us that passion and desire are unholy and that having them is a sin.
On behalf of myself and my generational line, I repent for all those who called what You call Holy, unholy and what You call unholy, Holy.

Prayers for Generational Freedom

On behalf of myself and my generational line, I repent for all those who instead of moving from duty to delight in their walk of faith, they went from delight to duty.
I repent for all those who believed that the goal of morality was morality itself, instead of believing the truth that the goal of morality is Ecstasy in God, for we were intended and created to love God and be loved by Him.

On behalf of myself and my generational line, I repent for all those who taught that there was no higher aspiration in the Christian walk that to be nice, and therefore produced a generation of men and women whose greatest virtue is that they don't offend anyone.

I repent for all those who taught or believed that desire, zeal, and longing were a sin and not only shut down these aspects in their own life but taught others to do the same. And in doing so, they ceased hungering and thirsting altogether, therefore they could not hunger and thirst after righteousness and after God. ~ 2 ~

I repent and renounce for all those in my generational line who committed spiritual suicide, by killing off their desire, zeal, and longing. For by doing so they shut down and killed a part of their heart, soul, and spirit.

I repent for all those who allowed desire unfulfilled, love lost, wounds and scars of the past, and heartache to cause them to shut down parts of their heart, or shut down their heart altogether.
I repent for allowing pain to have its way and allowing it to cause me to shut down my heart, instead of opening it up to love again.

On behalf of myself and my generational line, I repent for all

those who traded their passion for apathy and indifference, and their zeal for passivity and numbness.
I repent for all those who buried or killed their passions, desires, and zeal; for we were made in the image of Jesus Christ and we bear His very nature, and He is a God of passion, desire, and zeal.
On behalf of myself and my generational line, I repent for all those who tried to attain Holiness through works and duty. And for all those who believed the lie that it was possible to live in true holiness without passion, desire, and zeal.

Lord, on behalf of myself and my generational line I repent for all those that treated You like an object of duty, rather than an object of desire and affection.
I repent for all those who came before You and spent time with You out of obligation, instead of coming because they desired and longed for Your presence, as well as desiring to want to spend time with You.
I repent for all those whose relationship with You was based on duty and obligation, instead of being based on love, intimacy, passion, desire, and zeal.

On behalf of myself and my generational line, I repent for all those who buried or hid their deepest desires and called it maturity.
I repent for all those who buried their desires, and without a deep burning desire of their own they were ruled and swayed by the desires and passions of others.

I repent on behalf of myself and my generational line for neglecting the inner fire, the desires, the longings, and the passions that God had placed in us, and therefore we damaged ourselves, we damaged the very core of our being in the process.

Prayers for Generational Freedom

Lord, on behalf of myself and my generational line I repent for all those who tried to quench their deepest yearnings and desires that only You God can fill, with romantic love, sex, drugs, and other earthly things.

I repent for all those who gave their desires and passions over to any object or any other being other than God, and thus became ensnared.
I repent and renounce for all generational addiction.
I repent for the idolatry that addiction led us into.
On behalf of myself and my generational line, I repent for all those who through their addiction worshiped objects of attachment, thereby preventing them from truly and freely worshiping God.
Lord, please come and break all chains of addiction off of me and my generational line.

On behalf of myself and my generational line, I repent for all those who did not watch over and guard their hearts, their desires, their dreams, their passions, and their zeal with a fierce love and vigilance.

On behalf of myself and my generational line, I repent for all those who did not fight to enter into the fullness of everything that God had intended for them.

I repent on behalf of myself and all those in my generational line who because they allowed pain to have its way in their life, they came to the conclusion that they did not want to live life to the fullest for it was too hard. And in doing so, they said: "We want to live a life less than what God intended, and we don't want to pay the price it would take in order to live a life of bliss and intimacy with Jesus". And by refusing to continuing fighting for the best and warring for our birthright in Christ we in fact killed or shut down our hearts, and in doing so we rejected Jesus, and in the process, we caused great damage to our heart, our body, our soul, and especially our spirit.

Lord, I repent for wanting and desiring less than all that You have for me and my generational line.
Lord, I repent for pretending that I'm happy with where I am, that I am happy with business as usual.
Lord, please teach us how to be content and discontent, full and hungry at the same time. ~ 3 ~

Lord, I ask that You would bring back to the surface any and all passions, desires, longings, and dreams that I have killed or buried.
Lord, please awaken and bring my heart back to life.
Lord, I ask that You would restore me spirit, soul, and body; bring me into the wholeness of Your Spirit.
Lord, please come and heal all the wounds, scars, and all damage to my body, soul, spirit, heart, mind, will, and emotions that came when I rejected, buried, or killed the desires, passions, zeal, and dreams that You put into me.
Lord, please cause the righteous desires within us to bloom and blossom into fulfillment, growing into a tree of bliss and life.

1. ~ ~
Proverbs 13:12
12 Hope deferred makes the heart sick,
But when desire is fulfilled, it is a tree of life. ~ **Amplified Bible** ~
2. ~ ~
Matthew 5:6
6 "Blessed {joyful, nourished by God's goodness} are those who hunger and thirst for righteousness {those who actively seek right standing with God}, for they will be {completely} satisfied. ~ **Amplified Bible** ~
3. ~ ~
Philippians 4:12b
12 Everywhere and in all things I have learned both to be full and to be hungry, ~ **NKJV** ~

Caleb Peterson

RENUNCIATION OF GENERATIONAL IDOLATRY
Caleb Peterson

This prayer was birthed through my own personal shortcomings. Several years ago God showed me how I was in idolatry. I thought that idolatry only consisted of kneeling before idols and carved images. He showed me that idolatry can be something as simple as having views of God that aren't true, and are unworthy of Him. He taught me that it all comes down to our image of God and who He is.

Our image of God is very important to our spiritual walk, it is essential to fulfilling our birthright. For without a clear and true picture of who God is, we will never truly discover who we are. Wrong views or images of God deeply affect our lives and our spiritual walk. So how exactly do they affect us?

1. Idolatry
The first way that wrong views of God effect our lives and our spiritual walk is that having wrong views of God is actually a form of idolatry. When we have wrong views of God it is idolatry in two ways.

The first way is when we have wrong views of God we are entertaining thoughts about Him that are not true, we are allowing thoughts of Him into our being that are unworthy of Him. We are seeing and picturing Him as less than He really is, and that is idolatry plain and simple. We are picturing images of this amazing Uncreated God that are in fact not who He is. And they taint our views of who God is. Now I don't think we will ever know everything about God, or see every aspect of who He is. He is too vast for us to ever see or know it all. But during our adventure of seeking to know Him in a deeper and deeper way, we sure don't want to harbor images of Him that are incorrect or unworthy of Him and His divine image.

The second way that wrong views of God are idolatry is our worship. When we have views of God that are not really Him, and we worship those views as part of God. We are actually in a way worshiping other gods. For we are worshiping something that is not really God, something that isn't part of His nature or character. We are revering and worshiping false views of God. When we worship false aspects of what we perceive God to be, we are actually worshiping idols. We aren't worshiping God, we are worshiping a false view of Him.

We must be very careful because we cannot out of pride, ignorance, or arrogance accept the notion that idolatry consists only of kneeling before or worshiping visible objects or kneeling before idols, carved images, or statues. And that therefore since we do not participate in these activities, and since we don't revere or worship other gods, that our hearts are free of all idolatry. The truth is that the very core and essence of idolatry is the entertainment of any and all thoughts about God that are unworthy of Him. So when we see God as less than what He is, or we think of Him as less than He really is, that is absolute heresy, blasphemy, dishonor, disrespect, and last but certainly not least it is idolatry.

We need to see God as He truly is, we can't allow our imagination or our thoughts to lead us into false views of God. Nor can we allow the thoughts, opinions, or the views of others to sway us into thinking He is less than He is.

Romans 1:21-23

21 because, although they knew God, they did not glorify Him as God, nor were thankful, but became futile in their thoughts, and their foolish hearts were darkened.

22 Professing to be wise, they became fools,
23 and changed the glory of the incorruptible God into an image made like corruptible man – and birds and four-footed animals and creeping things. ~ NKJV ~

Now we are not changing the glory of God into images of birds and four-footed animals, but by entertaining thoughts and views of God that are unworthy of Him, we are changing and tainting the image and the glory of the incorruptible God. For we are viewing and thinking of Him less than He really is. Therefore we are tainting His perfect and flawless image in our minds, souls, and hearts.

As we see in scripture these wrong views of God actually darken our hearts. They knew God but did not glorify Him or worship Him as such. They thought up foolish ideas of what God was like, therefore their hearts were darkened. Wrong ideas and views of God darken and defile our hearts, which doesn't just affect us.

John 7:38

38 He who believes in Me {who cleaves to, and trusts in, and relies on Me}, as the Scriptures has said, From his innermost being shall flow {continuously} springs and rivers of living water. ~ AMPC ~

He who believes in Jesus as the scripture has said, then rivers and springs of living water will flow from his heart. So when we entertain thoughts of God that are unworthy of Him, our hearts are darkened which in turn pollutes the rivers flowing from our hearts. Our darkened hearts pollute the pure waters that flow within us and from our innermost being.

When the image of God that we have in our image center is something other than what He really is, it distorts our thinking and darkens our hearts. And if these false images of God are left undealt with and are not replaced with a true and righteous picture of what and who God really is, they will grow and pollute our thoughts, our hearts, and the water that flows from our hearts. So then not only do these false images of God affect us, but this polluted water flows out of us and affects the people around us.

Another way wrong views of God affects us is that we become what we see God as.

2 Corinthians 3:18

18 But we all, with unveiled face, beholding as in a mirror the glory of the Lord, are being transformed into the same image from glory to glory, just as by the Spirit of the Lord. ~ NKJV ~

What you see God as is what you will become. For we are beholding as in a mirror the image of God and are being transformed into the same image. The image that we have in our hearts and in our image center of what God is like, is what we will become. That is one of the reasons our perception of God is so very important.

So in order to get free of these false views, first off we need to ask God to reveal any and all thoughts or views of Him that we hold that are wrong. Then we need to invite and allow the Holy Spirit to deal with any and all thoughts, images, or views of God that are unworthy of Him. And not only teach us what God is really like but also draw us into a deep intimate relationship where we experience God's nature firsthand.

John 14:26

26 But the helper, the Holy Spirit, whom the Father will send in My name, He will teach you all things, and bring to your remembrance all things that I said to you. ~ NKJV ~

John 16:13a

13 However, when He, the Spirit of truth, has come, He will guide you into all truth; ~ NKJV ~

When the Spirit of Truth comes, He will guide us into all truth. When that truth comes it destroys all wrong views, thoughts, and mindsets in our being. This is something we desperately need. We must seek the Holy Spirit to teach us right views and mindsets of God, and ask Him to purge our lives of all idolatry.

~ PRAYER ~
RENUNCIATION OF GENERATIONAL IDOLATRY

I repent and renounce for all generational idolatry.
I renounce and repent for all idolatry, whether of the body, mind, or of the heart.
I repent for all generational unrighteous reverence.
I repent for all those who revered idols, other gods, or unrighteous spiritual beings.

I repent for all generational cultist worship.
I repent for all those who created religious cults in order to lead others astray, blind them from the truth, or keep them from fulfilling their destiny in Christ.
I repent for all those who allowed cultist leaders or followers to blind them or brainwash them and lead them down paths that seemed good but in the end resulted in spiritual defilement and death.
I repent for all idolatry that resulted from following these cults and their unrighteous beliefs and doctrines.

I repent for all those who through worship attempted to embody the divine aspects of other gods.

I repent for all those who created unrighteous religious systems, belief systems, doctrines, as well as creating other gods to follow and serve.

I repent for all those who entertained thoughts of God that were unworthy of Him.
I repent for all those who believed and entertained wrong views and mindsets of God, or about how He operates.

I repent and renounce for all those who revered and worshiped false aspects of God.

I repent and renounce for all those who created or taught false philosophies, doctrines, wrong views, or ideas about God.

I renounce and repent for all those who although they knew God, they did not glorify Him as God nor did they honor, treat, or worship Him as such.

Who were unthankful, and in turn became futile in their thoughts and their foolish undiscerning hearts were darkened.

Professing to be wise, they became fools and changed the glory of the incorruptible God into an image made like corruptible man, birds, four-footed animals, and creeping things.

Who exchanged the truth of God for falsehoods and lies, and who worshiped creatures of this earth rather than the Creator who created the heavens and the earth.

I repent and renounce for all generational stubbornness, which is as iniquity and idolatry.

I repent and renounce for all those in my generational line who served God halfheartedly and did not give Him their all. For, in essence, it is idolatry when God can't have every part of our being.

Lord, I ask that You would cleanse and illuminate our hearts that were darkened through our foolish sins.

Please cleanse the waters that flow within us from all contamination that came through our hearts being darkened by idolatry.

Lord, please remove any unrighteous substances, spirits, or beings that came upon us.

I ask that You would close any and all open doors, windows, gates, and portals that were opened that were not supposed to be opened.

Lord, please cleanse any and all unrighteous views and mindsets from my body, soul, spirit, mind, will, and emotions and replace them with righteous ones.

Holy Spirit please come and lead me into all truth.

Please envelope my being with the Spirit of Truth.

RENUNCIATION OF GENERATIONAL PREDATORISM
Caleb Peterson

There isn't much of a back story to this prayer. It came from seeing people operating in a predator spirit. Whether it was in my own personal life, or having to deal with it from my generational line. The predator spirit is a vicious circle. If you operate in the predator spirit and prey on others, then eventually the victim spirit will come upon you and you will become the hunted rather than the hunter.

We see this throughout history. The predator eventually becomes the hunted. It's something that is unavoidable. It's all part of God's Law.

Proverbs 22:8
8 He who sows iniquity will reap sorrow,
And the rod of his anger will fail. ~ NKJV ~

Galatians 6:7-8
7 Do not be deceived, God is not mocked; for whatever a man sows, that he will also reap.
8 For he who sows to his flesh will of the flesh reap corruption, but he who sows to the Spirit will of the Spirit reap everlasting life.
~ NKJV ~

Whatever a man sows that will he reap. If we sow wickedness we will reap wickedness. If we sow the predator spirit, that is what we will reap. If we prey on others sooner or later we become the prey. It's like putting a target on your back. Preying on others sets up and starts a physical and spiritual dynamic of a victim spirit coming over you, which of course results in predators seeking you out in order to attack you. It sets up a target on your back, and a spiritual tracking device on you so to speak.

This whole dynamic is something we need to repent of. And once this sin has been repented of we also need to ask God to break off not only the predator spirit but the victim spirit as well. And all the other unrighteous spirits and substances that came with them.

~ PRAYER ~
RENUNCIATION OF GENERATIONAL PREDATORISM

I repent and renounce for all those in my generational line who were predators, and victimized and preyed on any people group. Especially for all those who preyed on the innocent, which in turn allowed the victim spirit to come upon us. And we became the hunted instead of the hunters.

I repent for all those in my generational who were predators and preyed on others because of different skin color, culture, gender, beliefs, or religion.

I repent for all those who because of envy and jealousy attacked or preyed on others.

I repent and renounce for all those in my generational line who were predators and attacked and preyed on the innocent because they enjoyed stealing the innocence of others.

I repent for all those in my generational line who because their innocence had been stolen from them, they turned right around and stole the innocence of others.
I repent for all those who lost their own innocence and then attempted to replace it with the innocence of others.

I repent for all those who in my generational line who used unrighteous seduction, allurement, enticement, and temptation to steal the innocence of others.

I repent for all those who used witchcraft, sorcery, or any other occultic power to steal innocence.

I repent for all those who did not protect the defenseless and the innocent, even when they had the means to do so.
I repent for all those who because of pressure or not wanting to be victimized themselves, participated in the oppressing and preying on of the innocent.

I repent and renounce for all those who attacked or preyed on young children.

I repent for and I renounce all generational murder, massacre, torture and torment, physical and sexual abuse, rape, and all generational perversion.

I repent for all those in my generational line who used any unrighteous source or power to attack or prey on others.
I repent for all those who ascended to the second heaven in order to gain power or help to prey on others.
Lord, please remove any part of me or my generational line that is stuck in the second heaven because of these sins.
Please cleanse all parts of me and my generational line that have been stuck in the second heaven. Cleanse them in Your blood and integrate them back where You want them to be.

I repent for all those who called upon the dead, demons, or any other unrighteous spiritual beings to attack or prey on others.
Lord, please break the consequences of these sins off of me and my generational line.

I repent for all those in my generational line who because of fear or any other reason, invited or allowed others to prey on their family and did not protect them like they should have. And for all those who actually participated in the attacking and preying on of family members.

Lord, I repent on behalf of myself and my generational line for inviting or allowing the predator spirit to come upon us.
I repent and renounce on behalf of myself and my generational line for any time we allowed the predator spirit to operate in or through us, and for any time we attacked or preyed on others.
I repent for all those who preyed on others, which in turn brought on the consequences of us being preyed on.

I repent on behalf of myself and my generational line that because we were attacked and preyed on, we allowed the victim spirit to come upon us. And we camped in places of passivity and self-pity and would not defend ourselves.

I repent for and renounce all generational passivity, lack of courage, and lack of boldness that allowed predators to prey on and victimize us.

I repent on behalf of myself and my generational line for not fighting for our inheritance, and for not warring to possess our birthright, but instead, we were passive and scared and allowed the enemy to steal our inheritance and take our birthright.
Lord, please bring back everything that the enemy has stolen from us, or that we foolishly gave away.

I repent on behalf of myself and my generational line for the way we reacted when we were preyed upon. When attacked instead of turning to God to heal us and help us to walk in forgiveness; we grew cold allowing bitterness to consume us and then we turned right around and started attacking and preying on others.

I repent for all those who grew bitter after being preyed on and took vengeance into their own hands, forgive us, Lord, for You said vengeance is Yours. ~ 1 ~

Lord, please break off of me and my generational line the predator and the victim spirit.

Lord, forgive us for holding onto unforgiveness and allowing bitterness and resentment to consume us.

Lord, I now choose to forgive all those who attacked and preyed upon me and my generational line. I now release them to You to judge and release justice upon them.

Lord, I ask that You would remove any part of me or my generational line that is stuck in any place in the unrighteous depth, any unrighteous heavenly place, any place in the unrighteous deep, or any other unrighteous place.

Lord, I ask that You would remove all unrighteous targets, as well as all unrighteous tracking devices that the enemy was allowed to place on me or my generational line, because of our sins.

Lord, please break off of me and my generational line all hatred, malice, unrighteous anger, bitterness, resentment, passivity, cowardice, and all lack of boldness, as well as anything else that came along with these unholy spirits.

Lord, I ask that You would break off and remove any spirit of fear, terror, or horror that came on us through these sins.

Lord, would You come and put into me and my generational line Your holy boldness and Your holy aggression so that we might take the kingdom by force.

Lord, please implant into me and my generational line Your Holy Spirit of gentleness, so that we might be balanced in all things.

Lord, forgive me and my generational line for not having the

strength or the will to resist the enemy's assault on us.
Lord, I declare that my generational line and I are warriors and that we will not allow the enemy to prey on or victimized us anymore.
I declare that I am no longer prey of the enemy.

I repent for all those who sought comfort and protection from all victimization, from any other source than You, God.
Lord, I declare that You are my Father, my Protector.
I trust in You and You alone.
Hide me in the cleft of Your rocks and in the shadow of Your wings.

Caleb Peterson

1. ~ ~
Deuteronomy 32:35
35 'Vengeance is Mine, and retribution,
In due time their foot will slip;
For the day of their disaster is at hand,
And their doom hurries to meet them.' ~ **Amplified Bible** ~
Romans 12:19
19 Beloved, never avenge yourselves, but leave the way open for God's wrath {and His judicial righteousness}; for it is written {in Scripture}, "Vengeance is Mine, I will repay," says the Lord. ~ **Amplified Bible** ~

PRAYER TO REMOVE ONE FROM THE DUNGEONS OF THE DEEP
Caleb Peterson

This prayer started through a dream. I won't go over the entire dream, but I'll give you a brief outline. In the dream, the Lord revealed to me that myself along with several other people I knew, were trapped in a dark dungeon-like place. At the end of the dream, I heard the Holy Spirit tell me I was trapped in the Dungeons of the Deep.

Now I had never heard of the Dungeons of the Deep before, so I didn't know where or what they were. So the first thing I did was bring the whole thing before the Lord in prayer. While in prayer I heard the Holy Spirit say, "They are below the depths". Now I knew about the depths through my training under Dr. Paul Cox and his ministry Aslan's Place. We learned that there were righteous and unrighteous depths and that parts of our being can be trapped and imprisoned in different places in the unrighteous depths. So through what I heard in prayer, I am certain theses dungeons are places under the unrighteous depths, and that parts of our being can be trapped and imprisoned in these dungeons.

I knew that I was going to have to do some exploratory research. So naturally, the first thing I did was search the Bible. I searched throughout scripture, looking for any mention of the dungeons of the deep, or if it mentioned dungeons at all. With guidance from the Holy Spirit, I found several verses that talk about dungeons and even some that talk about dungeons below the depths.

2 Peter 2:4

4 For God did not spare the angels who sinned; on the contrary, He put them in gloomy dungeons lower than Sheol to be held for judgment. ~ CJB ~

After reading this verse I knew that I was on to something. My gut told me that these were the dungeons from my dream. Now verse 4 tells us that there are dungeons lower than Sheol. Which if you search scripture you will find out that Sheol is a place in the unrighteous depths. So if Sheol is a place in the unrighteous depth, and these dungeons are lower than Sheol, than they are either in the depths, or they are even lower than the depths. Now I believe that the deep is lower than the depths. Which would explain the dream very well.

In 2 Peter it tells us that God threw the angels that sinned into these dungeons. He confined them and imprisoned them in these dungeons. So we see through this verse that these dungeons like most dungeons are places of punishment. I believe that the dungeons talked about in 2 Peter are the dungeons in my dream; the Dungeons of the Deep. They are dungeons below the very depths, deep beneath the depths of Sheol. So, through certain sins that we or our ancestors commit, or through incidents that happened to us. Parts of our being can be trapped and imprisoned in these dungeons.

Lamentations 3:53-56
53 They have cut off my life in the dungeon, and cast a stone upon me.
54 Waters flowed over mine head; then I said, I am cut off.
55 I called upon thy name, O Lord, out of the low dungeon.
56 Thou hast heard my voice: hide not thine ear at my breathing, at my cry. ~ KJV ~

Isaiah 42:7
7 To open blind eyes,
To bring out prisoners from the dungeon
And those who dwell in darkness from the prison. ~ NASB ~

Zechariah 9:11
11 Because of the covenant I made with you,
sealed with blood,
I will free your prisoners
from death in a waterless dungeon. ~ NLT ~
Zechariah 9:11
11 Also you, by the blood of your covenant,
I release your prisoners from {the dungeon,}
the cistern that has no water in it. ~ CJB ~

So I continued to seek God and pray about it. Asking Him for clues. This is what I believe He has taught me so far, and what I got from the dream. These dungeons not only hold those trapped from consequences of certain sins committed. They also hold prisoners of war, those awaiting trial, and those imprisoned for crimes committed. These dungeons are deep below the depths, but I also believe they are connected to certain places within the depths. I believe they are connected to darkness, deep darkness, and utter darkness. I also believe that they are connected with, if not directly connected to the underworld. That, of course, is just a feeling that I got while praying. I could, however, be wrong.

These dungeons are deep dark catacomb-like dungeons. They seem to be subterranean catacombs. In these dungeons, you can hear the rushing of ghostly hosts, the cries of the tormented, and the eerie shrieks of the tormenting spirits. You can hear the clanking of chains as the prisoners' wail and attempt to get free. These dungeons are places of absolute torture and torment, and pain and agony. They are places of darkness and gloom. I could see and hear all this in my dream, it was pure agony just hearing the cries of pain.

These dungeons are waterless. Which of course has a direct effect on the prisoners, and while in these dungeons individuals become wells without liquid, dry cisterns yearning for water. These dark dungeons sap us of all water. We become dry, dusty wells that once contained refreshing life-giving water.

I continued to pray about it, trying to figure out more. One night I was spending time with God and I felt the Holy Spirit direct me to a verse in Matthew.

Matthew 18:34
34 And his lord was wroth, and delivered him to the tormentors, till he should pay all that was due unto him. ~ KJV ~

After reading this verse, I'm pretty sure that the Holy Spirit was telling me that the dungeons of the deep are one of the places of torment talked about in Matthew, if not the main place. Unforgiveness comes into our lives, and if we allow it to stay, it places us into these waterless dungeons and turns us over to the tormentors.

After some more prayer, I begin to sense I was missing something. So I sent this prayer to a friend of mine whom I trust. She read through the prayer and encouraged me that I was going in the right direction, but that she felt more needed to be added to the prayer. Her sense was that there were courts within these dungeons where people were tried and given unrighteous sentences. Courts where unrighteous charges and accusations were placed upon us. This, of course, made sense and lined up with notes I had made in the past. She also mentioned that she felt the presence of the court jester somehow. As she said this I got a picture in my mind of the court jester sitting in a judge's seat, presiding over trials in the deep. He sat there as dark beings acted as lawyers hurling false charges and accusations at the defendants. He wore a wicked smile on his face, evil laughter proceeding from his lips as he passed sentences down on these prisoners. Most were innocent of the crimes that they had been charged with, for false charges and accusations had been filed against them.

So naturally, I immediately started working on a

prayer to free myself and others from these dark dungeons, as well as dealing with the aspect of the courts and the jester. The following prayer is the result. I have seen this prayer make a huge impact not only in my own personal life but in the lives of several others. I pray it does the same for you.

Caleb Peterson

~ PRAYER ~
PRAYER TO REMOVE ONE FROM THE DUNGEONS OF THE DEEP

On behalf of myself and my generational line, I repent for and I totally renounce all generational unrighteousness, corruption, depravity, immorality, and wickedness.

I repent and renounce for all generational lust, uncleanness, and impurity.
I repent for and I renounce all generational lewdness, looseness, and indecency.

I repent and renounce for all those in my generational line who were pastors, ministers, clergymen, reverends, rabbis, teachers, and instructors; and created or produced false doctrines, teachings, principles, and religious systems. And because of wickedness or because of ignorance taught these false doctrines and false teachings to others.
I repent for all those who taught absolute heresy.
I repent and renounce for all generational false prophecy, and for all those who knowingly or unknowingly operated in false prophecy.
I repent for all those who were pastors and leaders and operated in false prophecy or allowed it to operate in their midst, without correcting or stopping it.

I repent and renounce for all those in my generational line who through wicked practices and sinful activities enticed other to walk immoral and unholy paths.
I repent for all those who used sexual practices to entice and lure the innocent into sin, evil, and the lusts of the flesh.

I repent and renounce for all those who allured and seduced others through the lusts of the flesh.
I repent and renounce for all those who debauched others by seducing them from chastity and led them away from purity and virtue.

I repent for all those in my generational line who love the wages of sin, wickedness, and unrighteousness.
I repent for all those in my generational line who were false prophets and false teachers, who were springs without water and mists driven by the tempest.
I repent for all those who uttered arrogant or vain words, words of deception masked and disguised to sound wise and profound, but in reality contained absolutely no life or spiritual truth, as well as substances of defilement.
I repent for all those who beguiled and lured others using lustful desires that pleased the eyes, but in the end brought death.
I repent and renounce for all those who promised others freedom, but could not give it for they themselves were slaves of sin, depravity, and corruption.
I repent for all those who allowed sin to defeat and overcome them, and therefore they were given over to and enslaved by sin.
I repent for all those who escaped the pollutions of this world, but later on were once again entangled and overcome by them. ~ 1 ~
Lord, please break the consequences of these sins off of me and my generational line.

I repent and renounce for all generational adultery.
I repent for all those in my generational line who drank water from cisterns other than their own, and running water from other wells'.
I repent for all those who did not rejoice and enjoy the

spouse of their youth, and instead enjoyed others. ~ 2 ~
I repent for all generational covetousness.

I repent and renounce for all those in my generational line who desired, craved, sought after, coveted, and took unto themselves other people's spouses. ~ 3 ~

I repent and renounce for all those in my generational line who came into union with any unrighteous spiritual beings for any purpose and brought upon themselves the consequences of being trapped and imprisoned in the Dungeons of the Deep.

I repent and renounce for all those in my generational line who openly defied or denied the Lord Most High, Jesus Christ.
I renounce and repent for all those who blasphemed against the truth, Spirit of Truth, of the Holy Spirit.

I repent and renounce for all those in my generational line who walked according to the flesh, instead of walking according to the Spirit.

I repent and renounce for all those in my generational line who had eyes that were full of sexual wickedness, that couldn't cease from sin and who had hearts trained in covetous, envious, and jealous practices. ~ 4 ~

I repent and renounce for all those in my generational line who forsook the right way, and who forsook the righteous path before them. And for all those who caused others to do the same.

I repent and renounce all generational lawlessness.
I repent for all those who despised and disrespected

authority of any kind.

I repent and renounce for all those who were presumptuous and overstepped their due bounds, and took liberties they shouldn't have.

I repent and renounce for all those in my generational line who slandered, disrespected, dishonored, and spoke evil of authority figures, dignitaries, and for all those who slandered any cosmic hierarchy, or any other unrighteous spiritual beings or spiritual dignitaries.

I repent and renounce for all those who would not yield to the wishes or orders of others, and would only be governed by themselves and their own will.

Lord, please break off of me and my generational line the curse of being wells without water, or being dry cisterns.

Lord, cause me to be a well of living water, a fountain springing up, a cistern full and overflowing with Your very living waters.

For I was created to be Your spring, Your fountain of living water.~ 5 ~

Lord, please break off of me and my generational line the curse of being doomed to utter darkness forever.

Lord, You said that unto the upright that a light would arise in the darkness, I ask that the light of Your countenance would arise upon us. ~ 6 ~

Lord, I ask that You would break all chains, irons, and shackles that are chaining me to any place in the Dungeons of the Deep.

Please disconnect me from any person or being that is empowering my imprisonment in these dungeons.

Lord, I ask that You would come and remove any part of me that is in any unrighteous place that is connected to the Dungeons of the Deep, especially the Underworld.

And cleanse these newly freed parts of my being in Your blood.
Lord, because of the covenant that You have made with me that is sealed in Your Blood, I ask that You would free any and all parts of me from these waterless dungeons. ~ 7 ~
Lord, please come and pull out and remove any and all parts of my being that have been trapped and imprisoned in the Dungeons of the Deep, and cleanse all parts of me in Your blood.
Lord, please bring back these parts back to me and integrate them into my being as they were meant to be, and align me spirit, soul, and body with You and Your plumb line.
Lord, please remove all tracking devices and any other such devices that were placed on my being.
Bring my entire being out of the darkness and into Your light.

~ Courts of the Deep ~

Lord, I ask that You would revoke all charges that have been brought against me and my generational line, that have brought about the consequences of being imprisoned in the Dungeons of the Deep.
Lord, please break off all unrighteous verdicts that have been placed upon me from any unrighteous court, judge, jury, or jester within or connected to the Dungeons of the Deep.

Lord, I ask that You would remove any part of my being that is being held for trial in the Courts of the Deep, please break the chains holding me in this unrighteous place and pull me out.
Lord Jesus, I ask that You would make null and void all charges, verdicts, accusations, decisions, decrees, or sentences that were passed down over me by the court

jester, the fool who calls himself the judge of the Courts of the Deep.

Lord, please disconnect me from these unrighteous courts, as well as the court jester residing over them and over my trial.

Lord Jesus, I ask that You would overturn all unrighteous charges and verdicts that have been placed upon me or my generational line, especially all those passed down by the court jester.

Lord, I ask that You would cleanse me spirit, soul, and body from all unrighteous verdicts, accusations, charges, decisions, or decrees, and from any and all curses or defilement that came with them.

Lord, please disconnect my entire being from any unrighteous courtroom, or judicial system in the Dungeons of the Deep, and from any judge, jury, or jester therein.

Lord, I ask that any and all accusations, charges, verdicts, and sentences that have been placed against me and my generational line would be brought before Your holy court.

Jesus, I ask that You would render a verdict of blessing and compassion as I throw myself at the mercy of the court.

Lord, please render a verdict of justice upon my enemies. Bring justice upon those who have brought trumped-up charges, false accusations, and unrighteous verdicts against me and my generational line.

Lord, I ask that You would once again cause the Rivers of Justice to flow not only through me and my generational line but through Your people Oh God.

Lord, I ask that You would break all curses off of us that came through our imprisonment in the dungeons of the deep, especially the curse of being waterless vessels.

Lord, cause us to overflow with the waters of justice. Cause the rivers that flow from our being to be infused with Your righteous, pure justice.

Lord, forgive me and my generational line for any time that we refused to extend the forgiveness that You had shown us to others.

Forgive us for any time that we held on to and harbored unforgiveness.

Lord, I ask that You would remove from me and my generational line all verdicts and sentences that came upon us because we would not extend forgiveness, and instead, we let resentment and bitterness grow in our hearts.

Lord, please remove any part of my being from any places of torture and torment, that the enemy was allowed to imprison us in because we held on to unforgiveness.

Lord, I ask that You would cleanse me spirit, soul, body, mind, will, and emotions from all unforgiveness, resentment, and bitterness.

Lord, please disconnect me from these unrighteous places and the tormentors therein.

Prayers for Generational Freedom

1. ~ ~
2 Peter 2:17-20
17 These are wells without water, clouds carried by the tempest, for whom is reserved the blackness of darkness forever.
18 For when they speak great swelling words of emptiness, they allure through the lusts of the flesh, through lewdness, the ones who have actually escaped from those who live in error.
19 While they promise them liberty, they themselves are slaves of corruption; for by whom a person is overcome, by him also he is brought into bondage.
20 For if, after they have escaped the pollutions of the world through the knowledge of the Lord and Savior Jesus Christ, they are again entangled in them and overcome, the latter end is worse for them than the beginning. ~ **NKJV** ~

2. ~ ~
Proverbs 5:15
15 Drink water from your own cistern,
And running water from your own well. ~ **NKJV** ~

3. ~ ~
Exodus 20:17
17 "You shall not covet {that is, selfishly desire and attempt to acquire} your neighbor's house; you shall not covet your neighbor's wife, or his male servant, or his female servant, or his ox, or his donkey, or anything that belongs to your neighbor." ~ **Amplified Bible** ~

3. ~ ~
Deuteronomy 5:21
21 'You shall not covet your neighbor's wife; and you shall not desire your neighbor's house, his field, his male servant, his female servant, his ox, his donkey, or anything that is your neighbor's.' ~ **NKJV** ~

4. ~ ~
2 Peter 2:14
4 having eyes full of adultery and that cannot cease from sin, enticing unstable souls. They have a heart trained in covetous practices, and are accursed children. ~ **NKJV** ~

5. ~ ~
Song of Solomon 4:12
12 A garden enclosed
Is my sister, my spouse,
A spring shut up,
A fountain sealed. ~ **NKJV** ~

5. ~ ~
Song of Solomon 4:15

15 A fountain of gardens,
A well of living waters,
And streams from Lebanon. ~ **NKJV** ~

6. ~ ~
Psalms 112:4
4 Unto the upright there arises a light in the darkness;
He is gracious, and full of compassion, and righteous. ~ **NKJV** ~

6. ~ ~
Psalms 4:6
6 There are many who say,
"Who will show us any good?"
Lord, lift up the light of Your countenance upon us. ~ **NKJV** ~

7. ~ ~
Zechariah 9:11
11 As for you also, because of the blood of My covenant with you {My chosen people, the covenant that was sealed with blood} I have freed your prisoners from the waterless pit. ~ **Amplified Bible** ~

Prayers for Generational Freedom

PHANTOM ZONE PRAYER
Caleb Peterson

I know I'm going to seem crazy through this one. If any of you are a comic book fan you have probably heard of this before. I am a huge Superman fan myself. And through him, I learned about the Phantom Zone.

Several years ago, I started to sense some sort of unrighteous enclosure around me. It seemed like I was in some sort of box, it felt cold and isolated. It looked to be made of glass. I couldn't figure out where I was. I wasn't getting any answers when I prayed about it. The answer to my inquiry came through my one of my favorite television shows: Smallville. A show about Superman's life. I was watching an episode and I saw Superman get trapped in a crystal box. A portal had been opened to the Phantom Zone, and he had been sucked in. This then became a crystal box and started traveling through space, till it reached the Phantom Zone and then it dumped him on the desert-like planet.

Now for those of you unfamiliar with the DC world. I will elaborate. The Phantom Zone is an alternate dimension that was discovered by the Kryptonian scientist Jor-El {Superman's Father}. Before Krypton's destruction, many of the nastiest criminals from the twenty-eight galaxies were imprisoned in the Phantom Zone. In most cases, these felons were mass murderers on a horrible scale, and the most horrific offenders were stripped of their physical bodies and flung into the Zone, becoming bodiless wraiths.

The Phantom Zone is a desert-like wasteland where the sun never sets, casting a dim gloomy haze over the planet. No forms of life have been shown to live or grow there, neither animals or plants. It is a dangerous prison, phantoms and wraiths roam freely, attacking other prisoners at will. The inhabitants are violent and angry, for being sentenced to a life on this hellish planet. Time has absolutely no meaning in this dimension.

I was pretty excited when this revelation started to come together. I love Superman, and to have God give me a revelation relating to this superhero was awesome. However, I know full well that a lot of Christians will think I'm crazy and off my rocker. But not only have I prayed through this prayer and experienced freedom in certain areas, I have had clients who have come back and brought good reports after praying through this prayer. So as the old saying goes, "The proof is in the pudding". And I have gotten to the point where I don't care what people think of the prayers I write. I'm not out to impress anyone. I'm out to walk in my birthright and destiny in God, and to please Him only.

Prayers for Generational Freedom

~ PRAYER ~
PHANTOM ZONE PRAYER

I repent and renounce for all those in my generational line who knowingly or unknowingly sent others into the Phantom Zone.

I repent for all those in my generational line who took on or tried to attack or battle unrighteous beings that they had not been instructed to by God, therefore they had no authority to do so and in turn, the enemy was allowed to trap parts of their being in the Phantom Zone.
I repent for all those who slandered, attacked, or came against any unrighteous hierarchy, which only succeeded in putting a target on their back and opened themselves up to attack.
I repent and renounce for all those who traveled to heavenly places, other dimensions, or alternate realms to battle the enemy without permission or instruction from God, and for all those who went into battle without heavenly strategies or wisdom from the Lord.

I repent and renounce for all those in my generational line who revered or worshiped phantoms or wraiths. ~ 1 ~
I repent for all those who used occultic means to send phantoms or wraiths upon others or upon their generational line.
I repent for all those who invited or allowed phantoms or wraiths to come in or upon themselves for any unrighteous purpose.

I repent and renounce on behalf of myself and my generational line for all those who came into unrighteous

union with any phantoms, wraiths, ghouls, or any other unrighteous spiritual beings.
Lord, please come and cleanse me and my generational lines blood and DNA from all contamination and defilement that came upon us and our blood line through these sins.

I repent and renounce for all those in my generational line who used unrighteous words, vibrations, rhythms, or music to exile or banish others to the Phantom Zone.
I repent for all those who used witchcraft, sorcery, any unrighteous rituals, or any other unrighteous means to open portals to the Phantom Zone.
I repent and renounce for all those who performed any blood or any other types of rituals to try and commune with any phantoms, wraiths, any other unrighteous spiritual beings, or any human being in the Phantom Zone.
I repent for all those who used animal or human blood in an attempt to open portals to the Phantom Zone or any other unrighteous place.

I renounce and repent for all those in my generational line who used any unrighteous bracelets, crystals, or any other piece of jewelry or token to open up portals to the Phantom Zone, in order to imprison others there. ~ 2 ~

Lord, if any part of my being is trapped in the crystal box traveling through space heading towards the Phantom Zone, please remove them and bring them back to me.
I ask that You would break, shatter, and destroy the crystal box that my sins, the sins or my ancestors, or that others have trapped me in.
Lord, please pull any part of my being out of any unrighteous places in space and time.

Lord, would you now come and with Your blood and open

the doorway to the Phantom Zone, and remove any and all parts of me being, or any part of my generational line that have been trapped or imprisoned there.

Lord, I ask that You would bring back to me all parts of my being that have been trapped in the Phantom Zone, wash them in Your blood cleansing them from all defilement.

Lord, please bring these parts back to me and integrate them back into my being where they are supposed to be.

Please align me spirit, soul, and body to Your righteous plumb line.

Lord, I ask that You would break all chains that are empowering my imprisonment in the Phantom Zone.

Lord, please break all ties and connections between me and any phantoms, wraiths, any other unrighteous spiritual beings, or any human being that are imprisoned in the Phantom Zone.

Lord, please remove any devices that were placed upon me in the Phantom Zone.

Lord, I ask that You would bring my entire being back into alignment with You and bring me out of any unrighteous time, bring my entire being back into right time and space.

~ 3 ~

Lord, I ask that nothing would be allowed to follow me out of the Phantom Zone, disconnect me from everything pertaining to this unrighteous realm.

Hide me in the shadow of Your wings, and remove any tracking devices of any kind.

Caleb Peterson

1. ~ ~

Resembling wraiths, phantoms are the bodiless form of the criminals sent to the prison known as the Phantom Zone. Making the Zone an absolute hell, they are constantly attacking and tormenting people trapped in the Phantom Zone. Even though they are primarily ghost-like, they are still able to cut, slice, and even grab their victims.

2. ~ ~

Phantom Zone bracelets originate from Krypton, and they open portals and entryways which in turn violently suck their victims into these open portals. The portal then becomes a crystal box which races into space until it reaches the Phantom Zone. It then opens another portal and drops its victim into the desert-like planet.

2. ~ ~

Crystals have the power to open portals to the Phantom Zone as well. They can be used as an entrance and as an exit. But it takes someone with extreme knowledge to do so.

3. ~ ~

Time has no meaning in the Phantom Zone, and anyone exiled or imprisoned there does not age and is trapped in a timeless limbo.

UNRIGHTEOUS SPIES AND WATCHERS PRAYER

Caleb Peterson

In several of my early sessions after I had graduated from Aslan's Place's internship. I began to see a recurring theme. I continued to discern unrighteous spies and watchers over the people I was praying for. They were spying on these people and reporting back to the enemy, allowing him to sabotage their plans and attack them in ways that hurt them right in their biggest weaknesses.

The Holy Spirit began to show me that we as Christians need to realize we are in a war. Now not only does our enemy not fight fair, but in every war, there are double agents and spies, as well as plants. Just to clarify, plants are people that look good, seem godly, and say all the right things, but the enemy placed them in our lives to either spy on us or to bring chaos and wreak havoc in our life.

We need to act like we are in a war. We need to rid our lives of any unrighteous spies, double agents, and plants. At times before we pray we need to ask God to close the eyes and ears of the enemy to all that we say and do. We need to act like we are in a war, and we need to take action to violently remove all unrighteous spies from our war camp.

For the enemy seeks to attain our marching plans, our war strategies, and our weaknesses. So he attempts to plant spies, watchers, double-agents, and plants in our midst, through our sins and just through the fact that we are at war. So I started seeking God on how to deal with these unrighteous spies and watchers over these people, and how to write a prayer for it. The following prayer is the result.

Caleb Peterson

~ PRAYER ~
UNRIGHTEOUS SPIES OR WATCHERS PRAYER

I repent for all those in my generational line who called upon or called up any unrighteous spies or watchers for the purpose of spying on others.
I repent for all those who prayed, chanted to, or worshiped these unrighteous beings.

I repent for all those who through evil practices, sent unrighteous spies or watchers on others, or on their generational line.
I repent for all those in my generational line who allowed or invited any unrighteous spies or watchers to come upon them and their generational line.

I repent for all those who used crystal balls, seer stones, or any other unrighteous device to spy on others, to steal their war strategies, or to watch their every move.

Lord, would You come and break any and all missions or assignments against any part of my being or my generational line, that have been given by the enemy or any human being.

Lord, I ask that You would break any and all ties and connections between me, my generational line and any unrighteous beings, especially any unrighteous beings that hold the title of a spy or watcher.

Lord, please come and remove any spying crows, or other watching fowl, and all birds of prey that have come over me and my generational line, because of our sins or because they were assigned to us by the enemy.

I repent for all those who lived in denial and refused to acknowledge that we are in a war.
I repent for all those who went about life living it in a business as usual attitude.

Lord, I ask that You would bring back any information that was stolen from us by any unrighteous spies or watchers. And I ask that You would erase all knowledge, info, blueprints, or maps that were stolen from us, from the enemies mind and remembrance.
Lord, I ask that You would hide me in the shadow of Your wings, and remove any unrighteous targets off of me and my generational line. Cover me and hide me in the cleft of the rocks, away from the prying eyes of the enemy.

Lord, I ask that You would take me and my generational line out of any unrighteous eyes.
Lord, would You please take me and my generational line out of any unrighteous place filled with eyes.
And please remove all unrighteous eyes that have been allowed to come upon, around, or in me.
And cleanse me from all defilement that came from these unrighteous beings.

Lord, I ask that You would remove all unrighteous spies and watchers from me and my generational line.
Lord, I repent for any time that I allowed spies into my midst, whether they were spiritual spies, or friends that I let into my inner circle when I shouldn't have.
I repent for not being discerning in the company that I keep, and the friends whom I let come around me.
Cleanse us from all defilement they brought upon us, and the fear they attempted to implant within our hearts.

Lord, please remove the unrighteous Watchers in the Night from me and my generational line.
Lord, I ask that You would shine Your light on the Watchers in the Night and the darkness surrounding them; breaking their power over me.

Lord, I now ask that You would restore unto me and my generational line all the righteous spiritual watchers that You intended to watch over us, as well as guard and protect us.
I command all fear, terror, and horror to leave me and my generational line now and go to the feet of Jesus.
Lord, I ask You to come as the Prince of Peace and bring Your peace that passes all understanding.
I also ask that You would come with Your perfect love, the only power that can reach the place where fear breeds. Come and root out all fear from every part of my being.

RIGHTEOUS INTIMACY PRAYER
Caleb Peterson

This all started off from research early on in my ministry. I had a few clients come for help and this came up more than once. I kept hearing the Holy Spirit saying something about seeking intimacy in the all wrong places. I started to discern that they or their ancestors had sought intimacy, love, and affection from unrighteous beings. They had been so wounded by people in their lives, that they no longer trusted people, and that opened a door for unrighteous beings to sneak in and offer love. It, of course, was false love and affection, but it at the time it felt better than the constant hurt and rejection they got from the people around them.

I knew that would cause more problems than the heartache they felt ever would. So I started seeking God to help me write a prayer to deal with this. First, off repenting for anytime we sought love in the wrong places and asking Him to cleanse us from the defilement that came with this sin.

Caleb Peterson

~ PRAYER ~
RIGHTEOUS INTIMACY PRAYER

I repent and renounce for all those in my generational line who sought love and intimacy from anything or anyone that they shouldn't have, especially all those who sought love and intimacy from any unrighteous spiritual beings.

I repent for all those who developed a close and intimate relationship with any unrighteous spiritual beings, and especially for all those who came into an unrighteous union with any unrighteous beings of any kind.
I repent for all those who allowed rejection, abandonment, and the pain of the past to cause them to walk into unrighteous relationships and unions.
Lord, please cleanse me and my generational line from any and all contamination that came through all unrighteous unions.

I repent and renounce on behalf of myself and my generational line for seeking love and intimacy from any unrighteous source rather than seeking it from You, Jesus.
Lord, please forgive us for seeking out love and intimacy in the wrong places and in the wrong ways.
I repent for chasing other lovers; for You are a jealous God and You will not share me with another. ~ 1 ~

I repent for all those in my generational line who sought the love and intimacy that they were supposed to get from You; from their spouse, family, or friends.
I repent and renounce for all those who sought the love and intimacy that they were supposed to get from You, through pornography or any unrighteous sexual relations.

I repent for any time that we loved our family, friends, or spouses more than we loved God. For when we did so we became unworthy of God. ~ 2 ~

I repent for all those who rejected the Love of God and instead accepted false love from the enemy.
I renounce all false love and false intimacy.
Lord, I ask You to remove all false love and false intimacy from my spirit, soul, body, heart, mind, will, and emotions along with the rest of my being.
Lord, please remove all false love from my generational line.
Lord, please fill me with Your holy love and intimacy, and teach me what true love looks like.
Lord, would You remove any and all contamination and defilement that came on me and my generational line, from us seeking love and intimacy from unrighteous sources, and from operating in or allowing false love to come over us.

Lord, would You close and seal all unrighteous doors that were opened through me or my ancestor's sins of seeking love and intimacy from any unrighteous source.
Lord, I ask that Your love would come and open the door to my heart that was closed to You through seeking love and intimacy from any unrighteous source.
For I hunger for Your holy love, intimacy, and affection.
I declare that true intimacy is what I am longing for.
I declare that true love and intimacy come from You and through You.
I now choose to give my all to You.
I declare I need You more than the very air I breathe.
You are a lover looking for a lover and that is why You created me.
Lord, I now choose to receive the love and intimacy that You have appropriated for me.
I claim that my spiritual birthright is that I am conceived in

love and that You chose me before the foundations of the world.
Lord, would You restore unto me and my generational line Your righteous love and intimacy.
For You created me for love and intimacy with You.
Lord, I ask that You would come and fill the longing in my heart. Come and fill the deep yearnings in my heart with Your love and affection. Come and touch the places deep within me that are aching with loneliness, and crying out for love.
Lord, I ask that You would remove anything and everything that keeps me from Your loving embrace.

Lord, would You cause me to dwell in the Secret Place of the Most High.
I declare that my birthright is to walk with You, Abba Father; in a close and intimate relationship. Where we walk hand in hand enjoying each other's company.
For I was made and created to dwell with You and to love You and be loved by You.
And I believe that Jesus Christ appropriated this intimacy for me when He ripped the veil in the Holy of Holies.

Lord, I repent for anyone in my generational line that tried to earn by works that which You had given freely by grace.
Lord, would You now usher me into that place of rest, love, intimacy, and perfect peace.
Lord, I ask that You would restore my relationship with You to what You intended it to be, so that I may enter into the love and intimacy with You that my heart aches for.

Prayers for Generational Freedom

1. ~ ~
Exodus 34:14
14 for you shall not worship any other god; for the Lord, whose name is Jealous, is a jealous {impassioned} God {demanding what is rightfully and uniquely His}-- ~ **Amplified Bible** ~

2. ~ ~
Matthew 10:37
37 He who loves father or mother more than Me is not worthy of Me. And he who loves son or daughter more than Me is not worthy of Me.
~ NKJV ~

Caleb Peterson

PRAYER TO BREAK THE CURSE OF UNRIGHTEOUS SINGLENESS

Caleb Peterson

The idea for this prayer came to me after reading an article by Arthur Burk. It was on singleness, and how there are a lot of Christians who desire a righteous mate but can't seem to find one. He mentioned that there had to be a spiritual component to this issue. My mind instantly went to a generational issue, which is how my mind works ever since God brought me into this ministry. My thoughts were that it had to be a generational curse somehow keeping these people from finding a spouse.

So I went before the Lord in prayer and asked Him to help me find the clues I needed to write a prayer to help people with this issue. This prayer is the result. I'm not saying I fixed the problem, or that this prayer will instantly break off everything holding individuals from finding someone, but I'm not saying it won't either. It might be different for different people. It might not be the entire jigsaw, but I think it is a piece.

~ PRAYER ~
PRAYER TO BREAK THE CURSE OF UNRIGHTEOUS SINGLENESS

I repent and renounce for all those in my generational line who used unrighteous power or the words of their mouths to curse others with singleness, and in doing so brought upon themselves the same curse.

I repent for all those who cursed others with roving and wandering, never being able to settle down and find a spouse.

I repent for all those who cursed entire generational lines with unrighteous singleness.

I repent for all those in my generational line who because of bitterness, spite, hatred, or because they were unable to find a spouse. They decided that no one else could have one either, so they cursed others with singleness.
I repent for all those who came into alignment with the Dog in the Manger mentality and operated in this unrighteous spirit.
I repent for all those who because they were miserable wanted everyone around them to be just as miserable as they were.

I repent for all those who because they were not happy they didn't want anyone else to be happy either.
I repent for all those who did not rejoice in the happiness of others and instead allowed anger, resentment, and bitterness to grow and fester within their hearts, at the sight

of friends, family members, and strangers in joyful loving relationships.

I repent for all those who allowed their actions to be dictated by jealousy and envy and refused to rejoice for the people in their life when they found someone special.

Lord, please forgive us for not rejoicing in the joy and happiness of others.

Lord, please break the consequences of these sins off of me and my generational line.

I repent and renounce for all those in my generational line who performed or participated in any rituals of witchcraft, sorcery, wizardry, black magic, voodoo, or any other unrighteous rituals that attempted or succeeded in cursing others with singleness.

I repent for all those in my generational line who knowingly or unknowingly cursed themselves or their generational line with singleness.

I repent and renounce for all those in my generational line who on purpose or by accident separated and tore apart married couples, therefore they came under a curse by breaking up what God had placed together.

Lord, forgive us and remove any and all curses that came upon us by breaking up what You had placed together, especially any curse of singleness.

I repent and renounce for all those in my generational line who performed or participated in any ritual sacrifices, with the body parts, organs, blood, or whole animals in any attempt to locate and find their soul mate.

I repent for all those in my generational line who used human organs or blood in any rituals, attempting to see into the future, for any prediction purposes, or to attempt to locate their future spouse.

I repent for all those who allowed loneliness and desperation to guide them and lead them down roads they were never meant to travel.

I repent for all those who because of loneliness and desperation turned to unrighteous things, people, or unrighteous spiritual beings for help and guidance in trying to find a spouse.

I repent and renounce for all those in my generational line who used spells, incantations, love potions, trances, charms, enchantments, or any other type of unrighteous force or power to find, locate, or hook a spouse.

I repent and renounce for all those in my generational line who performed or participated in any unrighteous rituals of trying to manipulate or influence time.

I repent and renounce for all those in my generational line who attempted to, or managed to warp or change the very fabric of time, as well as time and space.

I repent for all those who through evil practices sped up the timeline of their life, for the purpose of reaching the time when they would meet someone.

I repent for all those who performed or participated in any blood rites or rituals dedicated to any unrighteous beings of time.

I repent and renounce for all those in my generational line who made any covenants, oaths, or agreements with Father Time or any other unrighteous beings of time, in order to speed up the moments of their life.

I repent and renounce for all those who prayed or called upon Father Time or any other beings of time, in order to manipulate any change of time. And in doing so brought a curse upon the timeline of their lives, and a curse of time on themselves and their generational line.

Lord, please break the consequences of these sins off of me and my generational line.
Lord, please bring back any and all time that was stolen or given away.
Lord, I ask that You would cleanse the timeline of my life from all defilement, warping, and distortion.
Lord, please bring all warped or perverted time back into right alignment.

I repent and renounce on behalf of myself and my generational line for any and all sins that brought upon me and my generational line the curse of unrighteous singleness.

Lord, on behalf of myself and my generational line I choose to forgive all those who because of jealousy and envy cursed us.
Lord, please forgive us for any time we cursed others with singleness.

I repent for all those in my generational line who allowed the enemy to come in with his lies, and not only did they listen to them, but they also came into agreement and into alignment with these falsehoods.
I repent for all those who allowed the lies of the enemy to dictate their thought patterns, mindsets, and their actions. Causing them to do things they would never have done otherwise, thus opening the gates and doors of their life to the enemy. Which allowed him to come in with the curse of singleness and other evil.

I repent for and I renounce all vows, oaths, and agreements I made with my mouth, that God did not intend for me to make.
I repent for allowing the lies of the enemy to enter in, and to

dictate the words of my mouth.
I repent for not guarding the gate of my mouth and the door of my lips.
I renounce and reject the lie that God doesn't have a plan for my life.
I renounce and reject the lie that God doesn't have someone for me.
I renounce and reject the lie that I will never find someone.
I renounce and reject the lie that I will never find my counterpart.
I renounce and reject the lie that I will forever be alone.
I renounce and reject the lie that there is no one out there for me.
I renounce and reject the lie that I am not lovable, nor am I worthy of love.
I renounce and reject the lie that no one could ever love me for who I am.
I renounce and reject the lie that I will wander forever, never settling down.
I renounce and reject the lie that I am not good enough.
I renounce and reject the lie that I am not worth fighting for.

I renounce and reject the lies and falsehoods of the enemy.
And I now declare and proclaim the truth of God over my life.
I declare that God does have a plan for my life, to give me a future and to give me hope. ~ 1 ~
I declare that God does have a loving partner out there for me.
I declare that with the leading of the Holy Spirit I will find someone.
I declare that I will find my counterpart.
I declare that I will not forever be alone.
I declare that there is someone out there for me.

I declare that I am lovable and I am worthy of love.
I declare that there is someone out there for me, and they will love me for who I am.
I declare that I will not wander forever, and I will settle down and have a family.
I declare that I am worthy, that I am good enough.
I declare that I am worth fighting for.
And I decree and declare that in God's timing and in His way He will bring me the person He has for me. In His perfect timing, He will bring me the missing piece to my puzzle.

Lord, I ask that You would break, shatter, and destroy the curse of singleness off of me and my generational line, and any and all evil that came with this curse.
Lord, please remove any and all unrighteous beings, substances, or devices that the enemy was allowed to put in, around, or upon me that are being used to keep me from finding my future spouse.
Lord, please cleanse me and my generational line in Your blood, from any and all defilement.
Lord, I ask that You would cleanse the timeline of my life and bring every part of my being back into right time and order.
And I ask that You would bring time and space back into right alignment in my generational line, and cause us to walk and operate in Your righteous timing.
Please cleanse, adjust, and align my body clock, so that it will click and move, synchronized with You and Your perfect timing.
Lord, I ask that You would bring back to me and the timeline of my life anything that the enemy was allowed to steal; and close and seal all open doors, gates, windows, portals, or entryways, that the enemy has been allowed to enter and therefore access my life.
Lord, please restore everything that was stolen or given

away through our sins.

Lord, I decree and declare that I trust You and Your plan for my life. And I utterly reject all doubt, unbelief, and fear, especially of the future and what it holds.
I declare that I believe, Lord, heal my unbelief.
Lord, I ask that You would cleanse my spirit, soul, body, heart, mind, will, and emotions from all doubt, uncertainty, unbelief, and fear.
I love and I praise You, Lord Jesus; and no matter what happens I will choose to say, "The Lord is good and His love and mercy endures forever!"

1. ~ ~
Jeremiah 29:11
11 For I know the thoughts that I think toward you, says the Lord, thoughts of peace and not of evil, to give you a future and a hope.
~ NKJV ~

PRAYER TO BREAK UNRIGHTEOUS NETWORKS AND SETUPS BETWEEN SPOUSES

Caleb Peterson

This is another prayer I wrote after reading the article by Arthur Burk. After reading that article I went before God in prayer, asking Him to show me what exactly was keeping these righteous men and women from finding a good spouse. It was a bit self-motivated considering I was one of those people, but I also wanted to help others. So I wrote a few prayers that came while fellowshipping with God. In prayer I felt like something evil was between me and my future spouse, it seemed to be some sort of network. It looked like a huge structure of some sort, much like that of a wiring network or setup. So I begin crafting a prayer.

Like I said before I don't know if these prayers will help you find someone automatically or not. At this moment, I would say they are just a piece of the puzzle, but every little bit helps. It depends on where you are, what you have already dealt with, and what generational issues are in your generational line. I hope and pray these prayers bless and free you from that which is hindering your destiny from coming forth. And I hope and pray that all that is holding your future spouse from finding you is violently removed by the awesome hand of God.

Caleb Peterson

~ PRAYER ~
PRAYER TO BREAK UNRIGHTEOUS NETWORKS AND SETUPS BETWEEN SPOUSES

I repent for any and all sins that I or my ancestors committed that opened the gates, doors, and windows of my life and allowed the enemy to come in and create unrighteous networks, systems, databases, setups, or any other unrighteous structures of any kind between me and my future spouse.

Lord, please break, shatter, and destroy any unrighteous systems, setups, or networks connected by any wiring, communication lines, or electrical lines that are in between me and my future spouse.

Lord, please break, shatter, and destroy any unrighteous databases or structures connected by any cables, wiring, communication lines, electrical lines, or unholy ley-lines that the enemy has been allowed to put in between me and my future spouse. ~ 1 ~

Lord, please break, shatter, and destroy any unrighteous framework or structures that are between me and my future spouse.

Lord, please break, shatter, and destroy any unrighteous grids or electrodes consisting of mesh or fine wire, that are used as conductors of electricity or any other kind of unrighteous power, that are between me and my future spouse.

Lord, please break, shatter, and destroy any unrighteous transistors, terminals, or any other items or devices that emit or collect electrons and electricity; as well as controlling their movements, that are between me and my future spouse.

Lord, please break, shatter, and destroy any groups of unrighteous instruments or devices that have come together to form a system, database, structure, or network in between me and my future spouse.

Lord, please break, shatter, and destroy any unrighteous mechanical, automatic or robot-like machines, implements, instruments, or tools that the enemy has been allowed to plant in between me and my future spouse.

Lord, please break, shatter, and destroy any unrighteous electric, hydraulic, or any other type of machines that transmit power, force, motion, or energy to one another, that are between me and my future spouse.

Lord, please break, shatter, and destroy any assemblings or groups of unrighteous entities or beings that have come together to form a large system, database, structure, or network in between me and my future spouse.

Lord, please break, shatter, and destroy any unrighteous substance, matter, element, ingredient, compound, material, mixture, or composite that the enemy placed between me and my future spouse.

Lord, please break, shatter, and destroy any unrighteous vector, black hole, wormhole, space, or time that is in between me and my future spouse.

Lord, please break, shatter, and destroy any conductors for distribution of electrical or any other unrighteous power, that are between me and my future spouse.

Lord, please break, shatter, and destroy any unrighteous interconnected circuitry of cords, wires, or cables by which force is exerted to control or operate any mechanisms that are in between me and my future spouse.

Lord, please break, shatter, and destroy all unrighteous assemblages of electronic elements that create a path of electric current or power to any unrighteous source, that is in between me and my future spouse.

Lord, please break, shatter, and destroy any detailed plan or arrangement of electrical circuits, wires, or cables that are between me and my future spouse.

Lord, please break, shatter, and destroy any unrighteous spiritual or electrical maps, designs, or blueprints that the enemy has been allowed to not only put between me and my spouse but also put over my life in an attempt to distort my destiny and set me on an unrighteous path.
Lord, please cleanse me and my future spouse's life, destiny, and birthright from any and all defilement, and any power that attempts to control us through putting unrighteous maps and blueprints upon us, in order to project a false reality and destiny in front of us to follow.

Lord, please break, shatter, and destroy any unrighteous operation, activity, or work of the enemy that is going on between me and my future spouse.

Lord, I ask that You would come and remove any and all unrighteous systems, networks, databases, setups, structures, devices, transistors, terminals, substances, matter, machines, vectors, circuits, grids, maps, designs, blueprints, entities, or beings that are between me and my future spouse, that the enemy is using to keep us apart and keep us from finding each other.

Lord, please cleanse any and all ley-lines that are in between me and my future spouse, any ley-lines coming from the north, south, east, and the west.

Lord, please cleanse me and my future spouse from any and all defilement that came through these unrighteous setups and networks between us, and the enemy being allowed to mess with our relationship.

Lord, I ask that You would place all the righteous systems, databases, setups, structures, networks, devices, substances, matter, grids, maps, designs, blueprints, vectors, space and time, or any beings that You planned to be between me and my future spouse.

1. ~ ~

Ley-Lines were discovered by Alfred Watkins on June 30th, 1921. He had been going over a map when he discovered straight lines, pathways that ran over mountains and rough terrain. Every one of these strange pathways were ancient. Now at the time, Watkins didn't have a theory of what these lines or pathways were. Now later on after much study, he wrote his book, The Old Straight Track. In it, he sought to identify ancient paths and track-ways in the British landscape. His theory was that these ley-lines or pathways were ancient trade routes. He even said they were associated with the Greek God Hermes, {who was the god of trade, travelers, communications, boundaries, as well as being the guide that led travelers on unknown paths}. Now Watkins did not want to overreach in his theory as to what these lines were so he didn't go much further.

After his death speculations arose as to what these pathways actually were. Researchers have found that for the most part, these lines run pretty straight despite going over extremely rough terrain at times. They have been gone over by investigators and have been dated to 500-1200 AD. They have discovered that these were "Death Roads", that they were and some of them still are being used to transport the dead to their burial resting places. You can actually go online and look at maps of these lines over the US and the rest of the world. It's really quite fascinating.

Now we also believe that they were used in unrighteous ways and that they connect unrighteous points and were used to reach certain places used for sacrificial purposes. Now all of this science is great but what does scripture say about these lines? Does it mention them at all? Yes, I believe it does.

Isaiah 35:8

8 A highway will be there, and a roadway;
And it will be called the Holy Way.
The unclean will not travel on it,
But it will be for those who walk on the way {the redeemed};
And fools will not wander on it. ~ **Amplified Bible** ~

I believe that this scripture refers to spiritual highways that the Lord has established for us to walk upon. For us to move between dimensions and realms with His guidance of course. And that certain places people have tapped into the spirit realm seen where these highways go, and actually built physical pathways that lead right along with the spiritual ones. Usually this was done for unrighteous purposes.

So the question is if these are highways of holiness how did the enemy gain access to them? Well, we know that they enemy has no creative power within himself, so he cannot create anything for himself. All he can do is defile and use what the Lord has already created and established. So he corrupts the lines in order to utilize them for his own evil purposes. So it's quite possible that they enemy then uses these defiled lines for travel as well as communication. I know that some of you might ask how the enemy was able to defile these holy highways. Well in Genesis we see the sin of Adam and Eve. They disobey God's instructions and in doing so turn over the rule of creation over to Satan. So it is quite possible that these lines were also turned over to him.

But scripture tells us that we have the victory in God. And it talks about how all of creation groans awaiting its freedom.

Romans 8:19-22

19 For {even the whole} creation {all nature} waits eagerly for the children of God to be revealed.

20 For the creation was subjected to frustration and futility, not willingly {because of some intentional fault on its part}, but by the will of Him who subjected it, in hope

21 that the creation itself will also be freed from its bondage and decay {and gain entrance} into the glorious freedom of the children of God.

22 For we know that the whole creation has been moaning together as in the pains of childbirth until now. ~ **Amplified Bible** ~

Creation is groaning and anxiously awaiting the revealing of the Sons of God. It awaits the day when we arise into our positions as Sons of God and take back that which has been stolen from us. Take back the earth and all that is in the rule of the evil one. Cleanse it from all defilement and bring it into purity and freedom.

Now we can cleanse these highways right now in our own lives, homes, and properties. We do this by asking God to purify these holy highways. Now we should only do this on land or property that we have authority over. You can do this by walking the length and width of your house, land, etc... Asking God to cut off all contamination and defilement that the enemy was allowed to put on these lines.

Caleb Peterson

PRAYER TO REMOVE THE DOGS OF WAR

Caleb Peterson

This revelation was one of my most bizarre at the time. It was the first time God used the lyrics from a song to show me junk in a generational line. It all started in a session with one of my fairly regular clients. She was having trouble in the night time. Trouble sleeping as well as night terrors. So we had been digging looking for answers. Chipping away at the junk one session at a time. It seemed like there was no one thing responsible for the night terrors.

There seemed to be several things. So we were praying, asking God what He wanted to deal with in this session. As we sat there waiting the Lord brought a picture to her mind. It was a recurring dream that she had. A dream in which she was being chased by ferocious dogs; German Shepherds to be exact. They would chase her attempting to kill her, till they had her trapped on the top of a house roof. They would stay there at the base of the house, jumping and barking just waiting for her to fall. Then she would wake up.

As she was telling this dream I swore I could hear the snarling of a wild animal. So I knew we were on to something. But I could feel a very dark, nasty substance that I couldn't quite pinpoint what it was. I asked God what was going on and I heard the words, "Dogs of War". I asked my client if that meant anything to her and she said that it sounded like the title of a song, but she couldn't remember. So I googled it and lo and behold it was a song, Dogs of War by Pink Floyd. I was a bit flabbergasted. I am a pretty big Pink Floyd fan, I couldn't believe I'd never heard of it. So I looked it up on YouTube. As I pushed play I looked up the lyrics. I was a bit darker than most of their songs I was very surprised. But as I listened to it I felt the same substance that I felt on my client. As I read through the lyrics I found out what the substance was; it was the Spirit of Oblivion.

I could feel these dogs getting angry as they sensed us closing in on them. They were angry that we had found them out, as well as closing in on how to get rid of them. I asked the Holy Spirit to guide me in creating a prayer out of the lyrics right there on the spot. I wrote out a very rough draft and had her pray through it. When she did we both felt a shift. We could feel the dogs leaving, and with them the spirit of oblivion.

Then a few months later I was in a session with another client. I started to discern the exact same substance that I felt in my last session. But I couldn't feel the dogs of war. So we did a bit of exploring trying to figure it out. We went around and around but couldn't seem to figure out what was going on. I was starting to think I had discerned wrong and was about to give up. Then I felt a nudge from the Holy Spirit to go ahead and pray the prayer anyway. So I had her pray through it. As she began to pray through it I suddenly felt the presence of the dogs of war. Somehow they had hidden themselves in an attempt to go unseen and undealt with.

Somehow they had cloaked themselves so I wouldn't discern them and move on. As this was happening I could feel that she was in some sort of unrighteous place. It seemed to be a maze of catacombs where the dogs had been able to imprison her. They were able to lead her around in circles, causing her to be unable to move forward in certain areas of her life. As well as bring lies, falsehoods, and curses into her life.

Once we were done with the prayer I could see a change in her countenance. And I once again felt the same shift and the spirit of oblivion leaving her being. I was so excited, I had never gotten a prayer from a song before, but I knew it wouldn't be the last. I ended up finishing the prayer a few weeks later.

    I am extremely encouraged by the results I have seen from this prayer. I know a lot of people will think I'm crazy for writing a prayer from lyrics, but I feel like thanks to the Holy Spirit I'm on to something.

Prayers for Generational Freedom

~ PRAYER ~
PRAYER TO REMOVE THE DOGS OF WAR

I renounce and repent for all generational unrighteous anger, and all generational hatred.

I repent and renounce for all those in my generational line who wandered the land without a cause, and without discrimination; they slaughtered man, woman, and child.

I repent for all those who dealt in the currency of flesh and bone, as well as human blood.

I repent for all those who were cruel, ruthless, heartless, callous, cold-blooded, compassionless, inhumane, merciless, and malicious.

I repent for all those who through evil practices, unspeakable acts of wickedness, or rituals based in occultism; desensitized themselves, making themselves unfeeling and remorseless.

I repent for all those who were ruthless and because of their love of riches did anything for money.

I repent for all those who worked in falsehood, dishonesty, deception, and deceit.

I repent for all those who spun webs of lies, deception, and deceit.

I repent for all those who made any kind of transfers or business deals with any unrighteous beings.

I repent for all those who entered any unrighteous realms or dimensions in order to make deals with the enemy, which in turn brought death upon us and our generational line.

I repent for all those who entered these forbidden places and entered into deals with the enemy, which set off a chain of events that culminated in the Dogs of War being released and being allowed to hunt us down and deliver the spirit and substance of oblivion upon us.

Lord, please break off the curse that the Dogs will take and I must give, and that I must die so that they can live.
Lord, please break off any and all devices that steal and take life from my being.
Lord, please bring back everything that was stolen from me, cleansed in Your blood.
Lord, please break off the curse that causes the Dogs of War to not only follow me but to lead me around in circles, causing me to wander unable to advance forward.

Lord, I ask that You would remove the Dogs of War from me and my generational line.
I ask that all death and destruction would be removed from my being, as well as my generational line.
Lord, please bring back everything that was stolen from us, cleansed in Your blood.
Lord, please remove any part of me that is imprisoned in any unrighteous place, that the Dogs of War have me trapped in.
I rebuke and renounce, and Lord I ask that You would break the curse that no matter what I change or do the Dogs of War will remain.
Lord, please remove the spirit and substance of oblivion and all that came with it. Cleanse my spirit, soul, and body from all defilement that came from these evil beings and spirits.
Lord, I ask that You would close and seal all unrighteous gates, doors, windows, portals, and entryways that have

been opened over my life, allowing the enemy access to me and my generational line.

UNRIGHTEOUS SILENCE AND DARKNESS PRAYER

Caleb Peterson

This is the second prayer I have written that came from song lyrics. It all started when a small church group came to me for help. During one of their house meetings, they felt like something dark was attempting to silence their voices. So they started to pray about it. While taking it before the Lord in prayer one of them heard a song in their head. The song was Sound of Silence by Simon and Garfunkel.

So they came to me and asked me to write a prayer to help them out. Being the hardcore classic rock fan that I am, I had heard the song before. So I had a fairly good idea where to begin. But I try to never assume when it comes to these things. I always try to ask for the guidance of the Holy Spirit when I write prayers. So I began combing over the lyrics while in prayer. And the words began to come. The following prayer is the result of that time seeking God.

~ PRAYER ~
UNRIGHTEOUS SILENCE AND DARKNESS PRAYER

I repent and renounce for all those in my generational line who communicated with or made friends with unrighteous beings, especially the being Darkness.
I repent for all those who traveled to unrighteous realms or dimensions to communicate with any unrighteous beings for any purpose.

I repent and renounce for all those in my generational line who lived or dwelt in darkness.
I repent for all those who were imprisoned in darkness, deep darkness, or utter darkness and instead of fighting for their freedom and warring to return to the light, they grew content with their current situation. And they slid into despair and resignation and therefore remained in darkness.

I repent and renounce for all those who sought light in and from the darkness, as well as from other unrighteous sources.
I repent for all those who created unrighteous light and bowed before it, as well as worshiping it as god, instead of calling out to the Father of Lights, Jesus Christ.
I repent for all those who sought sustenance from these unrighteous lights, or false light gods or gods of light.
I repent for and I totally renounce any and all unrighteous religious systems that were born out of this unrighteous pursuit.

I repent and renounce for all those who did not closely

guard their dreams and invited or allowed the enemy in, which in turn allowed him to dictate their dreams or implant unrighteous seeds into different parts of their being.
Lord, please cleanse our imagination, and our dream life from any and all defilement of the enemy.

Lord, I ask that You would come and cleanse our physical and spiritual wombs from any and all defilement, as well as any unrighteous seed of the enemy.
Please come with Your holy fire and burn away all unrighteous seeds or bodily fluid that was implanted into us. Lord, please cleanse my blood, DNA, and RNA from all defilement.

Lord, I ask that You would break, shatter, and destroy any and all inception of the enemy.

I repent and renounce for all those in my generational line who were involved in any secret societies, especially those that had extreme consequences for breaking that vow of secrecy.
I repent and renounce for all those in my generational line who were involved in secret societies that forced their members into silence, and punished their members or their families if the silence was broken.

I repent for all those who lived in unrighteous silence.
I repent for all those who because of fear lived in silence, afraid to speak the truth concerned of the consequences that would follow.
Lord, please remove and cleanse us of all unrighteous silence and all the evil that came with it.

Lord, please remove any and all cancer like evil from our

beings that came from these sins, or from anything that the enemy was able to implant within us.

Lord, I ask that You would remove any unrighteous visions, dreams, thoughts, ideas, beliefs, images, imaginations, emotions, or feelings that were implanted in my brain, heart, mind, will, emotions, or any other place in my being.

Lord, please come and remove any and all parts of me and my generational line that are imprisoned, trapped, or are living in any part of the unrighteous depth, especially all those in darkness, deep darkness, and utter darkness.

Lord, please bring my entire being back into Your light.

Lord, I ask that You would cleanse these parts in Your blood and bring them back and integrate them back into my being where You intended them to be.

1. ~ ~
James 1:17
17 Every good thing given and every perfect gift is from above; it comes down from the Father of lights {the Creator and Sustainer of the heavens}, in whom there is no variation {no rising or settling} or shadow cast by His turning {for He is perfect and never changes}.
~ Amplified Bible ~

RENUNCIATION OF UNRIGHTEOUS ASPECTS OF THE CATHOLIC CHURCH
Caleb Peterson

One night I was in a small church group and different people were sharing how God was working in their lives. I don't remember how the topic came up, but one lady started talking about certain things people did in her Catholic church. One of the things she said really stuck out to me. She said that one of the biggest beliefs in the Catholic church is that they believe they are the mother church {so to speak} and that everyone outside their walls is a prodigal son that needs to return. That they believe salvation can only be found through them. And that they pray prayers that all prodigal sons and daughters would return.

After that I started to do some research of my own, to see if this was indeed fact. Everyone I talked to confirmed this belief along with several other disturbing ones. And then the Lord started to show me signs to confirm it even more. I began to suddenly see leaders in the church begin to join and come into alignment with the Catholic church. I could start to see the unrighteous pull that was happening.

Now please do not misunderstand me, I am not saying that the Catholic church is evil as well as all those in it. I'm not saying anything of the sort. I have met some very sweet people that are Catholic. Every denomination has views that are righteous, and views that are unrighteous. Every denomination had good and bad views. No one is perfect, and no denomination or religious system is perfect either. Every denomination thinks they are the entire pie when in truth all they have is one piece of the pie. It is when we finally come together as the Body of Christ and stop fighting each other, and we come together as one under Jesus and His mindsets and thoughts that we will have the whole pie.

And I'm not saying that everyone in the Catholic church is guilty of these things either, but we need to ask the Holy Spirit to search us and show us unrighteous mindsets that we hold. Not every Catholic is guilty of this, but it is real and it is happening. These prayers being prayed to bring others into the Catholic church are very controlling and manipulative. They are in fact Christian witchcraft. Any prayer that is prayed outside of the will of God is in fact witchcraft. And not everyone is supposed to be in or connected to the Catholic church. These unrighteous prayers have more effect that we think. They have an unrighteous pull that attempts to force people into this denomination. It's controlling, manipulative, and at its core extremely evil.

We need to repent of every time that we have attempted to pray prayers to bring others into the Catholic church or prayed any prayers that don't line up with the will of God. We also need to break the power of these words and all witchcraft off of ourselves.

That is where this prayer started, but through studying and the leading of the Holy Spirit, it grew to be a prayer of repentance from a lot more.

~ PRAYER ~
RENUNCIATION OF UNRIGHTEOUS ASPECTS OF THE CATHOLIC CHURCH

I repent and renounce for all generational unrighteous mindsets, especially all those connected to or aligned with the Catholic Church.

I repent for believing and coming into alignment with the belief that the Catholic church has power over the Bible and that the Pope can change times, abrogate laws, and dispense all things even the very precepts of Christ.
I repent for and I renounce the belief that the Catholic church cannot be bound by the authority of the Holy Scripture, and that they are entirely independent of the Bible. ~ 1 ~
Lord, I ask Your forgiveness for coming into alignment with these unrighteous mindsets, for no man is given the authority to change the Word of God.
Lord, You said that "Man shall not live by bread alone, but by every word that comes out of the mouth of God". ~ 2 ~
I declare that not only does Your word endure forever, but that it is sharper than any two-edged sword and cannot be suppressed or controlled. ~ 3 ~
I repent for all those who attempted to control, suppress, distort, or twist the Word of God.

I repent for believing and coming into alignment with the belief that Mary, mother of Jesus was sinless and that she was and is a co-redeemer with Christ. ~ 4 ~
Lord, I declare that You and You alone are our Redeemer and the Savior of all. ~ 5 ~

I repent for all those who prayed to or worshiped Mary instead of worshiping Jesus Christ the Lord of all. ~ 6 ~

I repent for and renounce all rosaries and repetitive duty filled prayers. ~ 7 ~

I repent and renounce for all belief that works and deeds brought grace, that in order to attain grace we must buy it with our labor and good deeds.

I repent for all belief that sacraments were a means by which God enacts His grace, as well as an outward sign of an inward grace. ~ 8 ~

I repent for the belief that these sacraments were necessary for salvation. ~ 9 ~

I repent for all those in my generational line who evaluated and placed their written traditions at the same level or above in stature and authority as the Word of God.

I repent for all those who believed that salvation could only be found in the Catholic church and that redemption and salvation could only be found within its walls. ~ 10 ~

I repent for and I totally renounce any and all unrighteous beliefs that the Catholic church is the only church that teaches the whole and complete truth.

I repent for and I totally renounce all generational belief that the Catholic church is the only place where God and the Holy Spirit dwell.
I repent for the belief that the Catholic church represents the whole church, as well as the entire body of Christ.

Prayers for Generational Freedom

I repent for and I renounce any and all belief that the Catholic church is the mother church, the one religion, the only way, and that all people outside of its walls are prodigal sons that must return in order to be in true fellowship with God.

I renounce and repent for all those who believe that all those outside of the Catholic church are lost, in sin, backsliders, and straying from the path of righteousness.

I repent and renounce for all those in my generational line who believed and aligned themselves with these unrighteous mindsets, and because of those beliefs used manipulation, coercion, or witchcraft prayers in order to bring people into the Catholic church.

Lord, I ask that You would break any and all unrighteous gravitational, electrical, or magnetic forces that are attempting to pull me and my generational line into the Catholic church.

Lord, I ask that You would break, shatter, and destroy any unrighteous tractor beams that are trying to pull me and my generational line into the Catholic church.

Lord, please break any and all unrighteous ropes, chains, or strings that are attempting to keep us connected to, or that are actively trying to pull us into the Catholic church.

Lord, please break, shatter, and destroy any and all unrighteous speech, words, decrees, declarations, edicts, pronouncements, proclamations, and judgments that have been spoken over me and my generational line by anyone connected to the Catholic church.

Lord, I ask that You would break, shatter, and destroy any and all curses, controlling prayers, and any Christian witchcraft off of me and my generational line.

Lord, please come and remove any and all unrighteous beings, spirits, matter, or substances that have come upon us through these unrighteous words.

Lord, please break off any unrighteous gear, clothing, devices or mechanisms, matter or substance, that attempts to control my mindsets or beliefs, especially those that attempt to change my beliefs and mindsets to align with those of the Catholic church.

Lord, please cleanse me spirit, soul, body, mind, will, and emotions from any unrighteous substance or defilement.

I decree and declare in the Name of the Lord Jesus Christ, that I will follow the directing of the Holy Godhead, no matter where they lead.

I will journey down the path that God has ordained for me, and that I will not allow the feelings and beliefs of others to dictate my spiritual birthright.

I declare that I do not have to be part of any denomination in order to grow closer to God or follow the path He has laid out before me.

Prayers for Generational Freedom

1. ~ ~
"The Pope has the power to change times, to abrogate laws, and to dispense with all things, even the precepts of Christ. The Pope has the authority and often exercised it, to dispense with the command of Christ."
{Decretal, de Tranlatic Episcop. (The Pope can modify divine law) Ferraris' Ecclesiastical Dictionary.}
"The authority of the Church could therefore not be bound to the authority of the Scriptures, because the church had changed the Sabbath into Sunday, not by command of Christ, but by its own authority."
{Canon and Tradition. Page 263}
"The doctrines of the Catholic Church are entirely independent of Holy Scripture."
{Familair Explanation of Catholic Doctrine. Rev. M Muller, page 151}

2. ~ ~
Matthew 4:4
4 But Jesus replied, "It is written and forever remains written, 'Man shall not live by bread alone, but by every word that comes out of the mouth of God.'" ~ **Amplified Bible** ~

3. ~ ~
Hebrews 4:12
12 For the word of God is living and active and full of power {making it operative, energizing, and effective}. It is sharper than any two-edged sword, penetrating as far as the division of the soul and spirit {the completeness of a person}, and of both joints and marrow {the deepest parts of our nature}, exposing and judging the very thoughts and intentions of the heart. ~ **Amplified Bible** ~

4. ~ ~
"That we may rightly say she (Mary) redeemed the human race together with Christ."
{Benedict XV, Inter Sodalicia, 1918}
"In fact, by being assumed into Heaven she (Mary) has not laid aside the office of salvation, but by the manifold intercession she continues to obtain for us the grace of eternal salvation."
{John Paul II, Dives in Misericordia, 1980, quoting Lumen Gentium}

5. ~ ~
Psalms 78:35
35 And they remembered that God was their rock, And the Most High God their Redeemer. ~ **Amplified Bible** ~
Isaiah 47:4
4 Our Redeemer {will do all this}, the Lord of Hosts is His name, The

Holy One of Israel. ~ **Amplified Bible** ~

6. ~ ~

"Let all the children of the Catholic Church, who are so very dear to us, hear these words of ours. With a still more ardent zeal for piety, religion, and love; let them continue to venerate, invoke and pray to the most Blessed Virgin Mary, Mother of God."
{Ineffabilis Deus, 1854, Pope Pius IX}

7. ~ ~

"To all those who shall pray my Rosary devoutly, I promise my special protection and great graces."
{Fifteen Promises of the Rosary}

7. ~ ~

Matthew 6:7

7 And when you pray, do not use vain repetitions as the heathen do. For they think that they will be heard for their many words.

~ **Amplified Bible** ~

8. ~ ~

A sacrament is a religious rite which has particular significance, especially in the Catholic Church. They consider the sacrament to be a visible symbol that God exists, as well as a way that He enacts his grace upon us. It's a symbolic rite that signifies God's grace in a way that is seen outwardly and can be observed by the participant.

9. ~ ~

"The Church affirms that for believers the sacraments of the New Covenant are necessary for salvation."
{Catholic Catechism}

10. ~ ~

"There is no salvation outside the church (Roman Catholic Church)."
{Pope John Paul II}

"Salvation is to be found nowhere but in the church (Roman Catholic Church), the strong and effective instrument of salvation is none other than the Roman Pontificate."
{Pope Leo XIII}

RENUNCIATION OF GENERATIONAL ANXIETY AND WORRY

Caleb Peterson

This prayer came from another request. A friend of mine asked if I would write a prayer to deal with personal and generational anxiety and worry. So, of course, I took on the challenge. I had dealt with anxiety and worry a lot in my own life, especially during my battle with self-hatred and depression. For both are a fairly big part of depression.

Anxiety and worry are far more deathly than we realize, and if left unchecked anxiety and worry will quickly begin to create depression in our lives. We see this clearly in scripture.

Proverbs 12:25
25 Anxiety in the heart of man causes depression,
But a good word makes it glad. ~ NKJV ~

So we see that anxiety can cause depression. When anxiety comes to us and enters our hearts, and we don't combat it and throw it out immediately, then it comes and sets up camp in our hearts and with it, it will bring depression, as well as other things. One of those things is worry. Which I believe is very closely connected with anxiety. I don't think you can experience one of them without the other. I truly believe that if you are dealing with anxiety then worry is not far off. It is usually hiding somewhere close by.

Now what is anxiety exactly and what does it do?
Anxiety;
1: fear or nervousness about what might happen.
2: a feeling of wanting to do something very much
3: a fearful concern

Now in scripture, we are told to be anxious about nothing.

Philippians 4:6
6 Be anxious for nothing, but in everything by prayer and supplication with thanksgiving let your requests be made know to God. ~ NASB ~

We are told very clearly in scripture what anxiety does to us, and we are told not to allow it into our lives. Now I truly believe that when anxiety comes it brings worry with it, for they are intertwined. I experienced this first hand in my own life and personal struggles. Of course, we all know what God says about worry. We see in Matthew 25 and in Luke 12 Jesus tell us not to worry about anything. What we will eat, what we will wear, etc... He feeds the fowl of the air, the young lions do not lack meat, so how much more will He take care of us.

Now while praying I felt like there was something else, like there was more to worry than I thought. So I started studying worry. First I looked it up in the dictionary.
Worry;
1: to think about problems or fears, to feel or show fear and concern because you think that something bad has happened or could happen.
2: to make {someone} anxious or upset, to cause {someone} to worry.
Its pretty straight forward, pretty much what I expected it to be, but as I studied a bit deeper something really caught my eye.

The old English for worry is "Wyrgan", which means "to strangle to choke". It was developed in 1670 from that of "harass by rough or severe treatment," like with dogs or wolves attacking a herd of sheep. It also means "to cause mental anguish and distress, to assail with rough or aggressive attack or treatment, or to torture".

This shocked me, so of course, I started digging even deeper. I went to the Strong's Concordance and began to study the word "worry".

In the Strong's "worry" is {merimnáō} which is an old verb for worry.

Merimnáō means;
A part, as opposed to the whole – properly, drawn in opposite directions; divided into parts. To go to pieces, to be pulled apart in different directions. Literally to be distracted, and to be divided.

Wow! So worry actually causes us to be pulled apart and divided. It comes and shatters us, it separates us into fragments. Possibly sending those parts to unrighteous dimensions, realms, and unrighteous heavenly places. Worry literally pulls us apart at the seams. When we allow worry to enter our lives it comes and creates havoc.

Peace in the Hebrew tongue is Shalom; which means nothing missing, nothing broken. So in essence worry is the exact opposite of peace. For worry breaks, shatters, and pull us apart at the seams. And very possibly sends these broken and shattered pieces into unrighteous dimensions, realms, and places. Now I truly believe that the Peace of God brings back to us pieces of our being that no other force can. So true Peace, real Shalom comes in and not only destroys the unrighteous authority that brings unrest, chaos, and confusion in our lives, but it also brings us into completion and wholeness.

As I look back at my own life I know that there have been multiple times when I have not only allowed worry into my life, but I have let it take over, taking a position of ruling over me. So not only was this prayer written for my friend, but for myself as well.

Caleb Peterson

~ PRAYER ~
RENUNCIATION OF GENERATIONAL ANXIETY AND WORRY

I renounce all generational stress, anxiety, and worry.

I repent and renounce for all those in my generational line who allowed anxiety, stress, and worry to dictate their thought patterns, mindsets, habits, schedule, sleep, as well as their lives.
I repent for all those who lived in anxiety and worry, instead of living in the Rest of God and dwelling in His peace.
I repent for allowing stress, anxiety, and worry to create confusion and chaos in our lives.
Lord, forgive us for allowing fear, anxiety, and worry to rule and dictate our lives, instead of living and dwelling in Your rest and perfect love.

I repent and renounce for all those who cursed others with stress, anxiety, or worry.

I renounce all depression connected with anxiety and worry.
I renounce all fear, terror, and horror connected with anxiety and worry.
I ask that You would come with Your flawless, perfect love that casts out and destroy all fear.
Lord, I ask that You would come with Your perfect love and reach deep down where fear breeds and remove it from me.

I renounce all stress, anxiety, and worry connected with the night, or any other time of the day, week, month, or year.
Lord, I ask that You would remove any and all unrighteous

beings that bring or create anxiety and worry from any part of my being.
Lord, please break, shatter, and destroy all ties and connections between me and these unrighteous beings.

I renounce all unrighteous ties and connections to the night, or any other time of the day, week, month, or year.
Lord, I renounce and I ask that You would break off any and all unrighteous effects the night has had on my heart, spirit, soul, body, mind, will, and emotions especially all those connected to anxiety and worry.

Lord, I repent for not combatting anxiety, worry, and stress as soon as they attempted to enter my heart, but instead, I allowed them to come in and take a place within my heart, bringing depression and other defilement.

Lord, I repent on behalf of myself and my generational line for allowing worry to come upon us and allowing it to stay in our minds, thus it was able to strangle and constrict not only our physical bodies but our spiritual ones as well.
I repent for allowing worry to infiltrate our beings, and then divide us, pulling us apart at the seams, shattering us in various areas of our lives.

I renounce stress, anxiety, and worry in all their forms.
I renounce all beings, spirits, and substances of anxiety and worry, especially any and all beings that create and generate these things.
Lord, I ask that You would come and take a high place of authority over every part of my life, and remove any and all spirits, substances, and beings that create or generate anxiety and worry that have been allowed to come over me and my generational line.

I command all stress, fear, anxiety, and worry to leave my spirit, soul, body, heart, mind, will, and emotions.

Lord Jesus, I ask that You would come as the Prince of Peace and wash over every part of me with wave after wave of Your peace that passes all understanding. Washing away all chaos, anxiety, fear, stress, and worry from every cell, every atom, every fiber of my being.

Lord, I ask that You would come and bring back every piece of my being that worry shattered and scattered to other dimensions, realms, and heavenly places.

Lord, please cleanse these pieces of my being in Your blood, and I ask that You would bring me back together and heal every broken and shattered piece of me.

Lord, come with Your peace and bring back the broken pieces of my being that worry has been allowed to shatter and scatter to other dimensions.

Lord, wash over me with Your Shalom; nothing missing, nothing broken. Make me whole and complete in You.

RENUNCIATION OF REJECTING RIGHTEOUS MASCULINITY AND MALE PROTECTION

Caleb Peterson

This prayer was born from an idea from my a friend. She messaged me one day asking me if I could write a prayer for her. She had noticed a unrighteous pattern in her life as well as in a few female friends of hers. A pattern that left them open and vulnerable to spiritual and physical attacks from men. So naturally, I said I would try.

As I began praying about it I felt the leading of the Holy Spirit. I felt that this dynamic had been released because women had rejected the righteous protection of the men in their lives. And so this attack was allowed to follow the generational line because it had not been repented of and removed. I also discerned a very strong connection to feminism and the female empowerment movement. I felt a very dark presence as I prayed through it. Then I began to see a picture of a huge dragon, very sinister in nature. I felt like it was a female dragon.

I inquired of the Holy Spirit who this dragon was and why she was here. I heard the name Feminism. I then knew this dragon's name and that she had something to do with this unrighteous dynamic. I then saw that in her hand she held the end of hundreds of chains, and at the other end were hundreds and thousands of women in shackles. I got the sense that this dragon had blinded these women and defiled them through unrighteous mindsets. These women had been shackled and imprisoned because they allowed these unrighteous mindsets to come over them and to rule their lives and dictate their actions.

So I started writing this prayer in order to break those chains and help those women find freedom.

~ PRAYER ~
RENUNCIATION OF REJECTING RIGHTEOUS MASCULINITY AND MALE PROTECTION

I repent for all generational hatred, rejection, or the control and suppression of righteous masculinity.

I repent on behalf of myself and all the women in my generational line for coming into alignment with and believing the lie of the enemy that if the men in their lives were to come into true masculinity that it would be a direct attack against their womanhood and their femininity.

I repent on behalf of myself and all the women in my generational line who attempted to suppress, squelch, silence, crush, trample, or tread upon masculinity in all its forms.

I repent for all the women who attempted to or succeeded in emasculating the men in their lives through physical, emotional, or spiritual means.

I repent for all the women who purposely squelched and suppressed the physical and spiritual leadership as well as the physical and spiritual giftings and anointings of the men in their lives.

I repent for all the mothers who because of fear or hatred of masculinity, suppressed their sons and would not allow them to grow into manhood or come into their birthright of masculinity.

I repent for all the women in my generational line who attempted to make the men in their lives ashamed to be male and tried to make them apologize for being a man.

I repent for all the women who taught young men that it was a sin to be a male, a sin to operate or walk in manhood or masculinity, and either forced them or manipulated them into repenting of their masculinity.

I repent for all the women in my generational line who refused to come into any level of submission to any form of masculinity, whether it was their father or their husband.
I repent for all the women who would not allow the men around them to lead or come into a place of leadership and authority; physically or spiritually.

I repent and renounce for all the women in my generational line who because of fear or because of despisement and hatred of masculinity, would not allow their husbands to step into the role of head of the household and instead took that role upon themselves.
I repent for all the women in my generational line who refused to submit to their husbands and instead took a role of power over their husbands squelching and completely suppressing them.
Lord, on behalf of myself and my generational line I repent for directly defying You and Your plan for marriage, by emasculating our husbands and stepping into the role of the leader and head of the household ourselves. And by doing so directly defied Your word. For You said, "Wives submit to your husbands, as to the Lord." ~ 1 ~
Lord, please break the consequences of these sins off of me and my generational line.

I repent on behalf of myself and the women in my generational line who because of hatred and fear; attacked, assaulted, and attempted to destroy masculinity in any of its forms.
I repent for all the women in my generational line who were

wounded and hurt by men, and instead of turning to You Lord for comfort and healing, they chose to revel in their pain and agony, and in turn sank into bitterness and hatred. Which caused them to despise and hate all forms of masculinity. And in order to never be hurt again, they took control and took the dominant lead of their relationships.

Lord, I repent on behalf of myself and all the women in my generational line who rejected, buried, or attempted to destroy any of the masculine parts of their soul, thus allowing the enemy to come and trap, imprison, and steal these soul parts in unrighteous places. ~ 2 ~
I repent for all the women who not only rejected the masculine parts of their soul but rejected all other forms of masculinity and turned to unrighteous acts, flaming with lust for one another.

I repent and renounce for all the women in my generational line who declared that they did not need, nor did they want the protection of a man, and therefore rejected the plan of God, which in turn opened the doors, gates, and windows of their lives to the enemy. Allowing him to set up a spiritual dynamic that brought about the consequences of physical and spiritual attacks.
I repent for all the women in my generational line who rejected righteous male protection from the men in their lives, as well as from God; opening themselves up to physical and spiritual attack.
I repent and renounce for all the women in my generational line who rejected the masculinity of God, as well as the male side of God.
I repent for all those who rejected God as their bridegroom and husband.
I repent for all the women in my generational line who rejected the headship and protection of God over their lives,

which not only left them open to attack but also allowed unrighteous beings to come over them and take a high place of authority over them.

Lord, I repent for all the women in my generational line who opened the gates, doors, or windows of their lives as well as the gates, doors, or windows of our generational line to the enemy through these unrighteous decisions.
Lord, I ask that You would close any and all gates, doors, or windows that have been opened because of our sins and our rejection of righteous masculinity, and all protection that comes with it.

As a member of this generational line, I decree and declare that I will contend against the bronze doors and iron bars in my life.
I also decree and declare that I and my descendants shall possess the gates of our enemies. ~ 3 ~

Lord, I ask that You would remove all hatred and fear of masculinity from me and my generational line.
Lord, please restore unto me and my generational line a pure respect, honor, and reverence for righteous manhood and righteous masculinity.

I repent for and I totally renounce all feminism.
I renounce all unrighteous beings, spirits, and substances that have come with my generational line's association with feminism.
Lord, please break off, shatter, and destroy all unrighteous ties and connections that were created from any association with feminism.
Lord, please cleanse my spirit, soul, and body from any and all defilement that came with this unrighteous spirit of feminism, and any unrighteous views, mindsets, or beliefs

that came with it.

Lord, please cleanse my spirit, soul, body, heart, mind, will, and emotions from any and all defilement that came from coming into alignment with these false beliefs.

Lord, please remove any and all unrighteous thoughts or mindsets in me and my generational line that came with aligning ourselves with feminism and hatred of masculinity.

Lord, I ask that You would come and remove any unrighteous being that has taken a high place of authority over me and my generational line.

Lord, I ask that You would come and remove the Dragon of Feminism that has taken a high place of authority over me and my generational line.

Lord, I ask that You would come and remove this Dragon off of the treasure that You placed within me before the foundations of the world.

Please remove this Dragon from her place of guarding the jewels of my heart and spirit.

Lord, as You are removing this Dragon from my treasure room and the wealth within, I ask that You would cleanse the treasure You have put in me, and the jewels of my heart and spirit from any and all defilement that has come from this unrighteous Dragon.

I also ask that You would remove any unrighteous treasure she may have brought with her.

Lord, please bring back any part of me or my treasure that was stolen from me.

Lord, I ask that You would remove any and all unrighteous flame from any part of my being.

Lord, please come and cleanse my treasure room from all defilement that was brought upon it through this unrighteous Dragon.

Holy Spirit, I invite You to come and inhabit my treasure

room; filling it with Your holy presence.

Lord, I ask that You would break, shatter, and destroy all unrighteous ties and connections between us and this Dragon, and any unrighteous being, spirit, or substance that she brought with her.
Lord, please remove the Dragon that has cloaked us in any unrighteous covering, along with the throne she sits on.
Lord, I ask and invite You to take Your rightful place as King and Bridegroom over me and my generational line.
Jesus, I ask that You would come as the Lion of Judah and take over the high place of authority over me, my treasure room, as well as over my entire generational line.

As a member of this generational line and as a woman, I decree and declare that I accept and invite back all the masculine parts of my being.
Lord, please cleanse all these parts and integrate them back into me, in correct and righteous alignment.

And as a member of this generational line and as a woman, I decree and declare that I accept the masculinity of God, and I declare that I will love and respect righteous masculinity in all its forms.
I declare that I do need righteous men and righteous masculinity in my life, and I accept righteous male protection, as well as the protection that comes from the male side of God.

Prayers for Generational Freedom

1. ~ ~
Ephesians 5:22-24
22 Wives, submit to your husbands, as to the Lord.
23 For the husband is head of the wife, as also Christ is head of the church; and He is the Savior of the body.
24 Therefore, just as the church is subject to Christ, so let the wives be to their husbands in everything. ~ **NKJV** ~

2. ~ ~
Yes, for the most part, God the Father, God the Son, and God the Holy Spirit are portrayed as male, but we know they have female aspects. For in Genesis we are told that both male and female were created in His image. So we know from that, that God is both masculine and feminine. We, of course, see lots of verses that talk about God as Father of all. But if you look you will also find verses that talk about God as a Mother.

Isaiah 66:13
13 As one whom his mother comforts,
So I will comfort you; you shall be comforted in Jerusalem. ~ **ESV** ~

Deuteronomy 32:11-12
11 "As an eagle that protects its nest,
That flutters over its young,
He spread out His wings and took them,
He carried them on His pinions.
12 "So the Lord along led him;
There was no foreign god with him. ~ **Amplified Bible** ~

So we see that God is both a mother and a father. So when He made man and woman He made them both in His image. So there are parts of both in us. Now the Motherly aspect of the Godhead I believe comes from the Holy Spirit.

We also see feminine aspects within certain names of God. The main one I want to focus on is; El-Shaddai.
Pronounced el shad-dy, it means "The All-Sufficient One" and is usually translated in English as "God Almighty".

~ ~ The Hebrew word "dai" means to {shed forth} or {pours out} which suggests provision and blessing. Thus, God is the All-Sufficient One

~ ~ The Hebrew word "shad" or "shaddayim" means breast or breasts and occurs 24 times as "Shaddai" and signifies One who nourishes, supplies, and satisfies. Combined with the word "El" it then becomes the One mighty to nourish, satisfy, and supply."

So we see that the Bible not only talks of God as a mother but also as the many breasted one. Our God is neither female nor male, for He is spirit, but within Him resides both masculinity and femininity. Males have within them some of both, the masculine parts of God as well as some of the feminine parts of God. And the same with women they have within them some of the feminine parts of God as well as some of the masculine parts of God. And none of us are the same, God knew what He was doing and he put different amounts of both in every male and every female. But through the fall when Adam and Eve sinned against God, and through our own sins these male and female parts can be defiled, twisted around, and certain parts that aren't created to take charge do. I have experienced this in my own life. And thanks to the leading of the Holy Spirit I found out and dealt with it. Yes, we both male and female have both male and female parts of our soul. But when we are male only male parts are supposed to be dominant and lead. And when we are female only female parts are supposed to be dominant and lead.

Now like we repented of in the prayer, through certain sins these parts can be trapped in certain unrighteous dimensions and realms. Not only that we can actively reject them because we don't want them or we feel they are in the way. We must not reject these parts of our soul, whether they be male or female. Each one is a wonderful part of who God created us to be. Now they may be damaged, defiled, or in the wrong place but that doesn't give us the right to reject them. We must take the steps needed in order to get these parts healed, cleansed, and back into right alignment within us. Every part God put into us is extremely valuable to who we are in Christ, to our spiritual and physical birthright.

3. ~ ~

Genesis 22:17
17 indeed I will greatly bless you, and I will greatly multiply your descendants like the stars of the heavens and like the sand on the seashore; and your seed shall possess the gate of their enemies {as conquerors}. ~ **Amplified Bible** ~

PRAYER OF REPENTANCE FOR DEMEANING THE DEATH, RESURRECTION, AND BLOOD OF JESUS CHRIST

Caleb Peterson

This revelation came from a word given by my younger brother. It came after a conference we attended. Something about that meeting had really grieved our spirit. I will not say who was speaking or where it was held, for I do not want to put anyone down or participate in gossip. But something was said about the crucifixion of Christ that had really grieved our spirits. We left trying to discern what was going on.

A friend who had been at the meeting called us to tell us he felt pretty much the same thing. We started praying about it, and an angel showed up with a message. My brother started getting a word. He started weeping and he said he could feel the wounded heart of Jesus. Jesus was grieved at some of the church's views on the crucifixion and what He endured that day. How some Christians downplay and minimize the extreme pain and agony He went through. How some Christians belittle the sacrifice He made for us, by preaching that He did not have to die on the cross. As well as downplaying what His death bought for us. You could feel the sadness of God in the very air. It felt like a thick fog in the car, so thick you could cut it with a knife.

In silence, I sat there, and under my breath, I began to repent for anytime I had come under this sin. Asking God's forgiveness for any time that I had operated in any unrighteous mindset that belittled or demeaned what He endured that day, and all that His sacrifice bought me. Asking Him to cleanse me of all unrighteous mindsets and views centered around His death and resurrection. Out of that quiet time of repentance, this prayer was birthed.

~ PRAYER ~
PRAYER OF REPENTANCE FOR DEMEANING THE DEATH, RESURRECTION, AND BLOOD OF JESUS CHRIST

Lord Jesus, I repent and renounce on behalf of myself and my generational line for all those that demeaned, belittled, and dishonored Your death and resurrection and all that it bought us.

I repent and renounce on behalf of myself and my generational line for all those who belittled and diminished what You endured on the cross, especially the physical and spiritual pain You went through on our behalf.

I repent for all those who created and taught doctrines that contradicted scripture by teaching that Jesus was so enraptured in the glory of the Father that He did not endure any pain on the cross.
I repent for all those who created and taught doctrines that contradicted scripture by teaching that Jesus did not have to die on the cross, in order to buy us our freedom.

I repent for all those who mocked, belittled, or demeaned all that You endured on my behalf that day;
~ The pain You endured even before the cross.
~ The bruises You took upon Yourself.
~ The pain of Your beard being ripped from Your face.
~ The pain of all Your bones being knocked out of place.
~ The stripes You took on Your back.
~ The pain of carrying the cross upon Your back as the blood drained from Your body.

~ The excruciating physical and spiritual pain You endured as You hung on the cross, bearing upon Yourself all the sin, iniquity, guilt, and shame of the world.

I repent and renounce on behalf of myself and my generational line for all those who demeaned and degraded the blood that You spilt and the immense power that it possesses.

I repent and renounce on behalf of myself and my generational line for all those who despised, scorned, or mocked Your holy blood, and for all those who reproached or challenged Your blood in a mocking or insulting manner.
I repent for all those who scoffed, gibed, or jeered at the Blood of Christ.
I repent for all those who viewed or treated the Blood of Christ with contempt or disdain.
I repent and renounce on behalf of myself and my generational line for all those who blasphemed or mocked the Lord's body and blood.
I repent and renounce for all those in my generational line who abhorred, loathed, and regarded the Blood of Christ with extreme hatred.
I repent and renounce on behalf of myself and my generational line for entertaining thoughts about the Blood of Christ that are not true, or that are unworthy of it and unworthy of Him.

I repent for all those in my generational line who attempted to warp, twist, or distort the true meaning and power of the Blood of Christ by teaching false doctrines and speaking lies about its true power.
I repent for all those who taught false doctrines created in order to debase and lower in honor the Blood of Christ in the eyes and hearts of others.

I repent and renounce for all those who did not approach communion with holy reverence and respect.

I renounce and repent on behalf of myself and my generational line for not rightly discerning the Body and Blood of Christ; and therefore were guilty of profaning and sinning against them, which brought a verdict of judgment upon ourselves and our generational line.

Lord, I come before You and as a member of this generational line, I repent for not revering Your body and blood, and for not rightly discerning them.

I repent for not rightly discerning the immense power of Your blood.

Lord, please break off any curse that came upon us because of this, and please forgive us and lift the judgment that was placed upon us. ~ 1 ~

Jesus on behalf of myself and my generational line I say "Thank You", for all that You endured on our behalf.

Lord, I ask that You would cause us to not only know about what You endured for us but that You would cause us to experience and partake of the suffering You endured on the cross.

Cause us to partake of the cup of Your suffering. That we might be glorified along with You and be called heirs of God and joint-heirs with Christ. ~ 2 ~

1. ~ ~
1 Corinthians 11:27-29 ~
27 So then whoever eats the bread and drinks the cup of the Lord in a way that is unworthy {of Him} will be guilty of {profaning and sinning against} the body and blood of the Lord.
28 Let a man {thoroughly} examine himself, and {only when he has done} so should he eat of the bread and drink of the cup.
29 For anyone who eats and drinks without discriminating and recognizing with due appreciation that {it is Christ's} body, eats and drinks a sentence {a verdict of judgment} upon himself.
~ **Amplified Bible** ~
2. ~ ~
Romans 8:17 ~
17 And if {we are His} children {then we are His} heirs also: heirs of God and fellow heirs with Christ {sharing His spiritual blessing and inheritance}, if indeed we share in His suffering so that we may also share in His glory. ~ **Amplified Bible** ~

PRAYER TO UNSEAT THE UNHOLY FEMALE TRINITY FROM OVER ME AND MY GENERATIONAL LINE

Caleb Peterson

This prayer started about nine years ago when the revelation for the unholy trinity came. I believe it all started with a dream, but it has been so long ago that the details of where it all started are a bit hazy. I remember coming into contact with this evil group a few times. They were operating through a few people I knew, but at the time I didn't know what they were. After seeking God for several months I finally started gaining some clarity. Here is what He showed me.

The members of this group are; The Dark Angel, Kali, and Jezebel. The Dark Angel is an Egyptian goddess {as well as a Native American goddess, for the Native Americans sometimes took on the gods and goddesses of other cultures as their own}, Kali is a Hindu goddess, and you all know about Jezebel. Now most of the time these three unholy female beings work alone, but at times they are allowed to come together to form a powerful entity, a powerful dominating, emasculating, feminist spirit. Which I call the Unholy Female Trinity. Now I did not just make that name up, I was given that name by the Holy Spirit.

At times they are allowed by our sins or the sins of our ancestors to come together over a person or their generational line. This entity is an extremely controlling, dominating, and emasculating force. That likes to come over women and prey on males through these women. There is a very strong male hating aspect to this entity, and I believe their goal is to destroy men in any way possible.

This entity is deeply rooted in female empowerment and feminism. It seeks to cause women to believe and come into agreement with certain lies.

The first lie is that the only way that women can protect themselves is to dominate in every aspect of their lives. Their work, their relationships, etc... There are several other lies connected to this unrighteous entity, all are dripping in male hatred and all of them seek to cause women to come into and operate in this hatred. And to destroy the male gender in any way they can.

Now when God brought this entity to my attention it was over a girl that I knew. She was extremely controlling and domineering. I could see it wasn't righteous in any way. So I began to ask God what was going on. When he opened my eyes to see this unrighteous trio over her, I knew I needed to know more. While in prayer I heard the words, Goddess Movement. So, of course, I did some research. This movement is a religion that grew out of the feminist movement. It was created because many women felt they were not being treated equally in many religions, and because they were deeply rooted in their feminist beliefs, they decided they needed a female deity. They wanted nothing to do with any male gods of any religion.

Most people within this goddess movement honor the triple goddess, the Maiden, the Mother, and the Crone. The Maiden aspect shows them how to be independent and strong, the Mother aspect shows them how to be nurturing, and the Crone aspect shows them how important it is to respect their elders. Each of these titles symbolizes both a separate stage in the female life cycle and a phase of the movements of the moon. Each one of these deities rules over one of the three realms; the earth, the underworld, and the heavens. Jezebel rules over the earthly realm, Kali the underworld, and the Dark Angel over the heavens.

The Maiden symbolizes and represents enchantment,

inception, expansion, the promise of new beginnings, birth, youth, and youthful zeal, and is supposed to represent the waxing moon. The Mother symbolizes and represents ripeness, fertility, sexuality, fulfillment, stableness, power, and life, and is supposed to represent the full moon. The Crone symbolizes and represents wisdom, rest, death, and endings, and is supposed to represent the waning moon.

The triple goddess is believed to represent unity, cooperation, and harmony for all creation, while male gods represent dissociation, chaos, separation, and domination. So of course here starts the hatred of the male side. They also believe that this is the original holy trinity; Maiden, Mother, and Crone. Now as I was studying this the Lord showed me that each goddess was connected to one of the titles. I believe that Jezebel is the Maiden, Kali the Mother, and the Dark Angel the Crone.

All this started a crazy journey of writing this prayer. I have had a few people pray through it with some amazing results. So I'm excited to see how God uses it to help deal with this unrighteous trinity.

Caleb Peterson

~ PRAYER ~
PRAYER TO UNSEAT THE UNHOLY FEMALE TRINITY FROM OVER ME AND MY GENERATIONAL LINE

1.0 Renunciation of Hindu Connections

I repent and renounce for all those in my generational line who revered and worshiped the Hindu goddess Kali, especially for all those who worshiped her as the Representer of the Void and the Destroyer of everything.
I repent for all the women in my generational line who revered and worshiped Kali as a symbol of feminine empowerment and feminine domination.
I repent and renounce for all the women in my generational line who worshiped Kali in her hatred and wrath against men.
I renounce the depiction of Kali dancing on and trampling her husband Shiva's dead body.

I repent and renounce for all the women in my generational line who came into alignment and agreement with Kali or any other male hating goddesses, spirits, or beings.
I repent and renounce for all the women in my generational line who came into union with Kali, or any other feminist goddesses, spirits, or beings.

I repent and renounce for all the women in my generational line who sacrificed males in any unrighteous rituals to worship, honor, or appease Kali or any other unrighteous spiritual beings.

I repent and renounce for all the women in my generational line who sacrificed male blood or any other male bodily fluids, to Kali or any other unrighteous spiritual beings.

I renounce and I repent for all blood rituals and blood sacrifices dedicated to Kali, because of the belief that she was only appeased with blood.

I repent and renounce all unrighteous blood covenants and oaths that I or my ancestors knowingly or unknowingly made with Kali, any other goddesses, or any other unrighteous spiritual beings.

Lord, please break, shatter, and destroy any and all blood covenants and oaths that I or my ancestors made with any feminist goddesses or spirits, as well as any male hating goddesses or spirits.

I repent for and I renounce all unrighteous beauty, unrighteous nakedness, unrighteous seduction, unrighteous allurement, and all false purity connected with Kali.

I renounce all domination against men, all control over men, all suppressing of the male spirit and male giftings, all trying to break the wild heart within them, as well as trying to crush the male spirit and dominate every aspect of their lives.

I repent and renounce for all those in my generational line who dedicated present and future generations to Kali, any other Hindu goddesses, or any other unrighteous spiritual beings.

I repent and renounce for all those in my generational line who worshiped the Hindu goddess, Shakti as the personification of the divine feminine creative power, and for all those who came into alignment or into union with her.

I renounce Shakti and her connection with Kali.

I renounce Kali and all her attributes, names, and titles.
Lord, please disconnect me and my generational line from Kali and all her attributes, names, and titles.
Lord, please disconnect me and my generational line from Shakti and all her attributes, names, and titles.
Lord, please disconnect me and my generational line from any other Hindu goddesses and their attributes, names, and titles.
Lord, I ask that You would disconnect me from any place in the underworld and bring back to me any part of my being that is trapped there, and cleanse them in Your blood.
Lord, please disconnect my entire being from any cycle of the moon especially the full moon.

I repent for and I totally renounce all despisement and hatred of men, as well as despisement and hatred of masculinity that came from our association with Kali.
Lord, please cleanse me and all the women in my generational line from all unrighteous substances and spirits that came upon us from our association with Kali, Shakti, any other Hindu goddesses, or any other unrighteous spiritual beings.

2.0 Renunciation of Babylonian Connections

I repent and renounce for all those in my generational line who revered and worshiped Jezebel, especially for all those who worshiped her as a symbol of feminine empowerment and female control and domination.

I repent and renounce for all those in my generational line who revered or worshiped Baal, and for all those who built temples or shrines dedicated to Baal.

Prayers for Generational Freedom

I repent and renounce for all those in my generational line who sacrificed males, male body parts, male blood, or any other male bodily fluid in any unrighteous rituals to worship, honor, or appease Jezebel, Baal, or any other Babylonian gods or goddesses.

I repent and renounce for all the women in my generational line who came into alignment or into agreement with Jezebel, or any male hating goddesses, spirits, or beings.

I repent and renounce for all the women in my generational line who came into any kind of union with Jezebel.

I repent and renounce for all the women in my generational line who were prostitutes and used their bodies to lead men astray or to control them.

I repent for and I totally renounce all generational adultery, fornication, sexual immorality, all temple prostitution, and all fertility rites.

I repent and renounce all blood covenants and oaths that I or my ancestors made with Jezebel or Baal.

I repent for and I renounce all unrighteous beauty, unrighteous nakedness, unrighteous seduction, unrighteous allurement, and all false purity connected with Jezebel.

I repent and renounce for all those in my generational line who dedicated present and future generations to Jezebel or Baal. Especially for all those who dedicated the females in their generational line; those born, and those yet to be born.

I renounce Jezebel and all her attributes, names, and titles.
Lord, please disconnect me and my generational line from Jezebel and all her attributes, names, and titles.
I renounce all emasculation spirits and substances that are connected to Jezebel.

Lord, I ask that You would remove any and all parts of my being that are trapped in any unrighteous dimension or place connected to this earthly realm. Bring them back to me cleansed in Your blood. Please break all ties and connections between me and these unrighteous places.
Lord, please disconnect every part of my being from any cycle of the moon, especially the waxing moon.

3.0 Renunciation of Egyptian Connections

I repent and renounce for all the women in my generational line who revered and worshiped the Dark Angel as the Egyptian blood goddess.
I repent for all the women in my generational line who worshiped her as a symbol of female domination.
I repent and renounce for all the women in my generational line who came into alignment with the Dark Angel and attacked and assaulted masculinity in any form.

I repent and renounce for all the women in my generational line who sacrificed men, male body parts, male blood, or any other male bodily fluids to the Dark Angel, any other Egyptian goddesses, or any other unrighteous spiritual beings.

I repent and renounce for all the women in my generational line who drained the blood from males, and used it for unrighteous purposes, or sacrificed it to the Dark Angel in any rituals to worship, honor, or appease her.

I repent and renounce for all the women in my generational line who used men or young boys in any rituals of fertility, rape, or any other sexual rituals.
I repent and renounce for all those who performed or participated in any rituals of rape, homosexuality, or any

other rituals of sexual immorality.

I repent for and I renounce all unrighteous beauty, unrighteous nakedness, unrighteous seduction, unrighteous allurement, and false purity connected to the Dark Angel.

I repent for and I renounce all fertility rites, all lust, eroticism, unrighteous passion, adultery, and sexual immorality connected to the Dark Angel.

I repent for and I totally renounce all despisement, hatred, and all controlling, suppressing, and dominating of the male gender.
I repent and renounce for all those in my generational line who dedicated present or future generations to the Dark Angel, especially the unborn females of our generational line.

Lord, I ask that You would remove, shatter, and destroy all networks and setups that the Dark Angel has been allowed to put over me and my generational line.

I renounce the Dark Angel and all her attributes, names, and titles.
Lord, please disconnect me and my generational line from the Dark Angel and all of her attributes, names, and titles.
Lord, please come and remove all substances of defilement, contamination, and evil that has come upon me and my generational line because of our sins and our association with the Dark Angel.

4.0 Renunciation of Native American Connections

I repent and renounce for all the women in my generational line who revered and worshiped the Dark Angel, as the

Native American blood goddess, especially for all those who worshiped her as a symbol of hatred of men and female domination.

I repent and renounce for all the Native Americans in my generational line who knowingly or unknowingly integrated with the worship of the Egyptians, Babylonians, or the Hindus; and worshiped their gods and goddesses. And for all those who used land dedicated to the deities of the Egyptians, Hindus, or the Babylonians and continued unrighteous practices of sacrifice and worship once performed on the land.

I repent for continuing to defile the land, instead of cleansing it in the Name of the One True God of creation; Jesus Christ.

I repent and renounce for all the women in my generational line who sacrificed men, male blood, or other male bodily fluids to the Dark Angel in her Native American aspect, or to any other Native American goddesses.

I repent and renounce for all unrighteous co-mingling of blood.
Lord, would You break any and all unrighteous soul ties, or any other unrighteous tie, connection, or bond that came through the co-mingling of our blood with any human being or any unrighteous spiritual being.

I repent for all those who made blood covenants with or to the land, with the Dark Angel, or any other unrighteous spiritual beings.
Lord, would You break all unrighteous blood covenants made by my ancestors and the consequences that came upon us because of these unrighteous covenants.

I repent and renounce for all the women in my generational line who performed or participated in any rituals of dancing on dead bodies, or in pools of male blood.

I repent and renounce for all the women in my generational line who drank or tasted male blood for the purpose of attempting to absorb the male spirit, male giftings, or the headship the Lord bestowed upon man.

I repent and renounce for all Native American blood, sacrifices, human sacrifices, or any other unrighteous sacrifices.

I repent and renounce for all the women in my generational line who sacrificed men, young boys, or male babies in any rituals of fertility, rituals dedicated to mother earth, or any rituals dedicated to the Dark Angel, or any other Native American goddesses.

I repent and renounce for all the women in my generational line who tortured or tormented males with fire, and for all those who burned them alive in any rituals.

I repent for and I renounce all unrighteous chanting or prayer to any of the Native American goddesses, Satan, demons, the dead, or to the Dark Angel.

Lord, would You break all unrighteous ties and connections between us and any unrighteous spiritual beings that came upon us through these sins.

I repent and renounce for all the women in my generational line who were involved in male massacre, slaughter, torture, torment, mutilation, scalping, head hunting, burning, rape, kidnapping, slavery, and unrighteous shedding of blood.

I renounce and repent on behalf of myself and those in my generational line who made unrighteous spiritual or cosmic

pacts or covenants between themselves and the land, the Dark Angel, or any other unrighteous spiritual beings.
Lord, would You break any unrighteous cosmic or spiritual ties, connections, or bonds, between me, my generational line and the land, or between us and the Dark Angel.

I renounce all hatred of men, all breaking of the male spirit, and all female domination connected with the Dark Angel.

Lord, please come and remove all substances and spirits of defilement, contamination, wickedness, and evil that has come upon me and my generational line because of our sins and our association with the Dark Angel. Cleanse me and my generational from all male hatred and despisement.
I renounce the Dark Angel as a Native American goddess, as well as all her attributes, names, and titles.
Lord, I ask that You would remove any and all parts of my being that are trapped in any unrighteous heavenly place. Please cleanse these parts of my being as You integrate them into my being. Please break any ties and connections between me and these unrighteous places.
Lord, please disconnect every part of my being from any cycle of the moon, especially the waning moon.

5.0 Renunciation of the Unholy Female Trinity

Heavenly Father, I repent and renounce on behalf of myself and the women in my generational line; for all hatred, despisement, contempt, mockery, condescension, malice, and dishonoring of men and what they carry.

I repent for all generational hatred of the male gender and of masculinity in all its forms.
I repent and renounce for all absolute domination and control of men by the women in my generational line.

I repent and renounce for all the women in my generational line who because of fear or hatred of masculinity or of men, they took over the place as head of the household and dominated and controlled the men in their lives.
I repent and renounce for all the women in my generational line who refused to come under any kind of male authority and refused to come into any type of submission.
I repent and renounce for all the women in my generational line who because of fear or hatred of masculinity, they rose up and took over the place as the head, and would not allow their husbands to step into their God-given role as head of the household.

I repent and renounce for all the women in my generational line who used sex and reproduction to try and manipulate, control, or dominate men.

I repent and renounce for all the pregnant women who prayed or chanted to Kali, Jezebel, or the Dark Angel, in an attempt to manipulate the gender of the baby in the womb.

I repent and renounce for all the women in my generational line who revered and worshiped Kali, Jezebel, the Dark Angel or the single greater divinity that they form when joined together.

I repent and renounce for all the women in my generational line who because of hatred of men turned away from Jesus Christ, and served other deities because they were female in gender.
I repent for all the women in my generational line who rejected the male parts of God, because of hatred and malice.
I repent and renounce for all the women in my generational line who were foolish and because of hatred of men turned

from Jesus Christ, and invited or allowed Kali, Jezebel, the Dark Angel, or the Unholy Female Trinity to be their master, shepherd, guide, and lord. Allowing them to lead them in this world and in the spirit realm.

Lord, please come and pull any part of me or my generational line out of the netherworld, the underworld, Hades, any place in the unrighteous depth, the unrighteous deep, or any other unrighteous place that Kali, Jezebel, the Dark Angel, or the Unholy Female Trinity have been allowed to lead us to and entrap us in.

I repent and renounce for all the women in my generational line who came into alignment with any male hating spirits, goddesses, or any feminist spirits or goddesses. Especially for all those who came into alignment or into union with the Unholy Female Trinity.

I repent and renounce for all the women in my generational line who came into alignment or into union with the Unholy Female Trinity and attacked and assaulted masculinity in any form.

I repent for all the women who attempted to put men beneath the soles of their feet.

I repent and renounce for all generational unrighteous female rule.

I repent and renounce for all the women in my generational line who were unrighteous priestesses and served false gods, and created unrighteous religious systems as well as false doctrines.

I repent and renounce for all the women in my generational line who believed and vowed that they didn't want or need men.

I repent and renounce for all the women in my generational line who because of their absolute hatred of men, turned

from God's original purpose and burned with desire, lusted after, and committed indecent acts with other women.
I repent for and I renounce all generational homosexuality in all its forms.

I repent and renounce for all the women in my generational line who sacrificed men in any unrighteous rituals to worship, honor, or appease the Unholy Female Trinity.

I repent and renounce for all cruelty, torture, and torment of men by the women in my generational line.
I repent and renounce for all the women in my generational line for all unrighteous violence, fury, and rampage against men.
I repent and renounce for all the women in my generational line who murdered men by hanging, burning, drowning, decapitation, disemboweling, dismemberment, mutilation, or by bleeding them to death.
I repent and renounce for all the women in my generational line who brutally murdered and slaughtered men for fun, pleasure, enjoyment, or because of pure hatred.
On behalf of myself and all the women in my generational line, I repent and renounce for all generational murder, mass murder, massacre, slaughter, genocide, carnage, and butchery of men.
I repent and renounce for all the women in my generational line who because of hatred tried to destroy, exterminate, and wipe out the male race.
I repent and renounce for all the women in my generational line who performed or participated in any unrighteous rituals of castrating and emasculating men physically and spiritually.

I repent and renounce for all the women who cut out men's tongues so they could silence them, and for all those who

tried to silence their spiritual voices.
I repent for all the women who physically or sexually abused the men in their lives.

I repent for all the women who tasted or drank male blood for any unrighteous purpose.
I repent and renounce for all the women who drained males of their blood and then bathed in the blood in an attempt to take the male spirit, soul, or the spiritual headship given to men by God upon themselves.

I repent and renounce for all blood covenants or oaths that I or my ancestors made with the Unholy Female Trinity.
I repent and renounce all blood rituals, all blood rites, all blood sacrifices, all unrighteous shedding of blood, all bloodletting, all mixing of wine and blood, all eating of flesh, all offering or eating of organs and heart, all cutting of the dead, all mutilation, all union with Kali, Jezebel, the Dark Angel, the Unholy Female Trinity, or any other unrighteous spiritual beings through blood rituals or covenants.
Lord, would You come and cleanse me and my generational line, and break all curses, agreements, covenants, oaths, and vows that I or my ancestors made with any unrighteous spiritual beings.

I repent and renounce for all those in my generational line who dedicated their generational line's blood or DNA to the Unholy Female Trinity, or any of its members.
Lord, would You cancel any and all right to access our blood or DNA that the enemy may have gained through our sins.
Lord, please close and seal any unrighteous portals, gates, doors, or windows that have been opened through our sins.
Lord, please cleanse our blood and DNA from any and all defilement that came as a result of our sins.
As a member of this generational line, I now take back our

blood and DNA that was dedicated or given away to any unrighteous sources, and I now dedicate our blood and DNA to the Lord, Jesus Christ.
Lord, please come and inhabit our very DNA.

I repent for all those who traded future blessings, giftings, and anointings that were not theirs to trade, for instant gratification and power.

I repent and renounce for all the women in my generational line who because of their innocence had been stolen from them by the men in their lives, they allowed anger and bitterness to consume them. And they turned right around and took revenge on men of all ages, stealing their innocence in any way they could.

I repent and renounce for all the women in my generational line who used witchcraft, sorcery, wizardry, voodoo, black magic, or any other occultic power to attack, victimize, or prey on men.
I repent and renounce for all generational divination.
I repent and renounce for all the women in my generational line who used male blood, body parts, or male babies in any rituals of divination or soothsaying.

I repent for and I renounce all generational enchantment, bewitchment, charming, spellbinding, and mesmerization.

I repent and renounce for all the women who used unrighteous charm, fascination, mesmerism, enchantment, bewitchment, spellbinding, hypnotism, witchcraft, sorcery, wizardry, voodoo, or black magic to attack, trap, control, or dominate men.

I repent and renounce for all the women who attempted to

manipulate or control the elemental spirits in an effort to control or dominate men.

I repent for and I renounce all unrighteous beauty, unrighteous nakedness, unrighteous seduction, unrighteous allurement, and false purity connected with the Unholy Female Trinity.

I repent for all those who enticed men to sin and entrapped them in unrighteous places by sexual or occultic means.

I repent on behalf of myself and all the women in my generational line for allowing any man hating spirits, predator spirits, or any other unrighteous spirits to come upon and operate through us.

Lord, I ask that You would come and break, shatter, and destroy all man hating spirits, all predator spirits, all hatred, malice, and anger towards men off of me and my generational line.
Lord, come and cleanse me and my generational line from all defilement and contamination that came with these unholy spirits.
Lord, come and cleanse my DNA, RNA, and every cell and atom of my being from all generational trauma, pain, unrighteous anger, bitterness, and all fear, terror, or hatred of the male gender.

Lord, I repent and renounce the lies and deceptions of the enemy that were placed within us by unrighteous sources.
I repent for and I renounce the lie that if the men in my life come into true masculinity that it will be an attack against me and my femininity and for all the evil actions that this lie led me and my ancestors into.
Lord, forgive us for allowing fear, deception, and the lies of

the enemy to dictate our thought patterns, our actions, and our lives.

Lord, I ask that You would come and break, shatter, and destroy any and all spirits or substances of deception, control, manipulation, hatred, unrighteous domination, emasculation, feminism, prejudice, unrighteous anger, and malice off of me and my generational line.

Lord, please come and cleanse me and my generational line from all unrighteous substances and spirits that came with the Unholy Female Trinity.

Lord, I ask that You would come and unseat and remove the Unholy Female Trinity from over me and my generational line, and remove any and all substances or spirits of defilement, and all effects or influences that they have had over me, my actions, my thought patterns, my mindsets, and my life.
Lord, please remove all other unrighteous spirits and beings that are connected with the Unholy Female Trinity that have been allowed to come over us.
Lord, I ask that You would replace them with the righteous female or male beings that You intended to be over me and my generational line.

Lord, please give me Your mind and feeling for the men in my life, cause my thoughts, views, and mindsets to alignment with Yours, and remove all lies and deceptions about men.
Lord, please remove from me and my generational line all fear and hatred of men.

Lord, I ask that You would come and cleanse me and the women in my generational line from any and all defilement that came upon us from our sins and our association with the Unholy Female Trinity.

Lord, I ask that You would break, shatter, and destroy any and all unrighteous networks or setups that the Unholy Female Trinity was allowed to put on me and the women in my generational line.
Lord, please come and implant into me and the women of my generational line a righteous and holy reverence for true masculinity and a righteous respect for the male gender.

PRAYER TO REMOVE KALI AND SHIVA FROM IN BETWEEN MARRIED COUPLES
Caleb Peterson

This prayer came about while trying to help a friend. He was having a lot of trouble in his marriage. He and his wife were not getting along and they were fighting a lot. They wanted help so they scheduled a session with me and my family. I request people schedule a session a week or more in advance so I can seek the Lord beforehand.

So one afternoon while in soaking prayer, I was seeking God to reveal what it was that was causing all this trouble. Searching for some clues to this situation. I begin to see a picture in my mind. I saw my friend and his wife and they were very angry at each other. They were fighting and arguing very loudly. I watched for a while then I felt like I was missing something. So I asked God what it was that I wasn't seeing. Then suddenly I saw a strange being between them, but they couldn't see this being. It seemed to be some sort of Hindu goddess.

It had 8 arms or so, and it would punch the wife and point to the husband blaming him. Then it would punch the husband and point to the wife blaming her. I started praying about it and got some help from a few friends of mine as well. After some research and prayer, I felt that the goddess was Kali. So, of course after learning that I started doing a lot of research on her. And I started writing a prayer to help while picking a friend's brains for help.

About a week later my friend and his wife canceled the session, saying they felt they could handle their problems on their own. So I let the matter go, and put the prayer away and forgot it for the time being. It didn't come back to my mind until several months later when my friend and his wife had filed for a divorce. I was pretty certain that the goddess I had seen between them was responsible, but of course, I couldn't be 100% sure. So once again I pushed the prayer out of my mind.

Then several years later another friend of mine was having problems in his marriage and was seeking help. As soon as I started praying about it the same image popped into my head. I saw that Hindu goddess between them and she was doing the same thing she did to the last couple. I was determined not to let this thing break up another couple. So I found the unfinished prayer, along with all my research and I went to work. I started going over my notes and praying through them. While in prayer I once again saw Kali doing the exact same thing she did to the last couple, but this time I could feel the presence of another. I couldn't figure out what I was discerning, so I called a friend of mine who knows a lot about Hindu stuff. She told me that if Kali was there her husband; Shiva had to be close by. A bell went off in my spirit, that was the clue I needed.

So, of course, I not only did some study on him I also picked my friends brain about all she knew about Shiva. A few weeks later I finished a rough draft of the prayer.

I went to my friend and told him what I had seen. So he and his wife set up an appointment with me. They kept the appointment, which is good! I ended up doing a session on both of them, having them both pray through the prayer.

Fast forward a few years and they are still together and doing much better. Now I wish I could say that I'm positive that this prayer did the trick, but I don't know that for certain. And I don't think I will ever know till I reach heaven and ask God. But it sure could have been the prayer, or the prayer and some other things. I do however know that Kali and Shiva are no longer between them causing trouble, which is a huge plus!

~ PRAYER~
PRAYER TO REMOVE KALI AND SHIVA FROM IN BETWEEN MARRIED COUPLES

I repent and renounce for all generational idolatry.
I repent and renounce for all those in my generational line who revered and worshiped Kali, Shiva, or any other of the Hindu gods and goddesses.

I repent for all those in my generational line who dedicated adults, children, babies in the womb, the uterus, the womb itself, or future generations to Kali, Shiva, or any other Hindu gods or goddesses.

I repent for all those who dedicated human eggs, sperm, or their reproductive organs to Kali, Shiva, or to any Hindu gods or goddesses.

I repent for all those in my generational line who used young girls or young boys in any rituals of fertility, rape or unrighteous nakedness, unrighteous seduction, unrighteous allurement, false purity, or any other rituals of sexual immorality to or for Kali or Shiva.

I repent and renounce for all those in my generational line who dedicated their marriage to Kali, Shiva, or any other Hindu gods or goddesses in any unrighteous wedding ceremonies or rituals.
I repent for all those who invited or allowed Kali or Shiva to officiate their wedding.
I repent for all those who dedicated their spouses to Kali, Shiva, or any other Hindu gods or goddesses.

I repent and renounce for all those who betrothed their young girls or young boys to Kali or Shiva.
I repent for all those who actually married Kali of Shiva.
I repent for all those in my generational line who forced their children into unrighteous marriages to honor or appease Kali and Shiva.
Lord, I ask that You would break all unrighteous betrothals and marriages that we made with unrighteous beings.
Lord, please break all unrighteous ties and connections that came with these unrighteous unions.

I repent and renounce for all those in my generational line who dedicated the honeymoon consummation, or their sex life to Kali, Shiva, or any other Hindu gods or goddesses.
I repent for all those who invited or allowed Kali of Shiva to come upon any part of their being during intercourse.

I repent and renounce for all those in my generational line who came into unrighteous union with Kali, Shiva, or any other Hindu gods or goddesses.
I repent on behalf of myself and my generational line for coming into unrighteous union with anything or anyone that the Lord did not intend for us to come into union with.
Lord, please break all unrighteous covenants we made by coming into these unrighteous unions.
Lord, please break the consequences of these sins off of me and my generational line.

Lord, I ask that You would come and cleanse me and my generational lines blood and DNA with Your fire and Your blood; from any defilement that came because of these unrighteous unions and because of our sexual sins.
Lord, please come and inhabit our very DNA, purging our veins with Your purity.
I repent and renounce for all those who prayed or chanted

to Kali or Shiva to try and manipulate the birthing process or the gender of the babies in the womb.

I repent for all the women in my generational line who invited Kali, or any other Hindu goddesses to come into their uterus and womb, in order that they could interfere with the babies blood, DNA, gender, or the birthing process.

I repent for all those who tried to manipulate time and space by praying or chanting to Kali.
I renounce all unrighteous time and all unrighteous timing associated with Kali.
Lord, please take me and my generational line out of any unrighteous time and bring us back into Your righteous timing.

I repent for all those in my generational line who sacrificed human eggs, sperm, blood, DNA, body parts, pregnant women, men, children, or babies to Kali, Shiva, or to any other Hindu gods or goddesses in any unrighteous rituals.

I repent and renounce for all blood sacrifices, blood covenants, or blood oaths made to Kail or Shiva.
I repent for and I renounce all unrighteous blood rituals, all blood rites, all blood sacrifices, all unrighteous shedding of blood, all bloodletting, all drinking and tasting of blood, all blood bathing, all mixing of wine and blood, and all eating of flesh, organs, or heart.
I repent for and I renounce all union with Kali and Shiva through blood rites, all offering or eating of organs and heart, all cutting of the dead, all mutilation, and all communion with Kali and Shiva.
Lord, I ask that You would cleanse me and my generational line from all defilement that came with these sins.
Lord, please break any and all curses, covenants, oaths,

vows, or agreements that I or my ancestors made with Kali, Shiva, or any other unrighteous spiritual beings.

I repent for all those in my generational line who performed or participated in any unrighteous rituals of rape, bestiality, homosexuality, or any other rituals of sexual immorality.

I repent for and I renounce all unrighteous beauty, unrighteous nakedness, unrighteous seduction, unrighteous allurement, and false purity connected with Kali and Shiva.
I renounce all sexual immorality.

I repent for all those who cursed themselves or their womb.
I repent for all those who used Hindu witchcraft rituals or ceremonies to curse women, their wombs, or the babies in the womb.
I repent and renounce for all those in my generational line who believed that Kali was the mother of the universe and the giver of life, worshiping her as such. Which in turn cursed the womb, causing death to come upon their physical and spiritual womb.
Lord, please come and break the spirit of death off of me and my generational line, and off of our physical and spiritual wombs.

I repent and renounce for all those in my generational line who revered and worshiped the Hindu goddess Kali as the eternal energy, the goddess of time and change, the force of time, the ultimate reality, the redeemer of the universe, the mother of the whole universe, the mother goddess, the one who terrorizes, the one who devours the hordes, the slayer of demons, the foremost among the ten Tantric goddesses, one of the seven tongues of Agni, the goddess of death, the queen of the dead, the queen of the damned, the black one, the great protector, the all-pure one, and any other of Kali's

attributes, names, or titles.
I renounce the Hindu goddess Kali in all her forms and depictions.
Lord, please disconnect me and my generational line from Kali and all her attributes, names, and titles.

I renounce Kali and the dark lion she rides on, and all the serpents and jackals that accompany her.
Lord, please remove all unrighteous serpents, jackals, lions and any other beings that have come upon me and my generational line because of sin, or association with Kali.
I renounce any and all jewelry or tokens that Kali wears or carries around with her, including the skull-topped staff, the garland made of human heads, her skirt made of human arms, her unrighteous sword, her unrighteous trident, and any other jewelry or tokens she bears.

I renounce all unrighteous roaring connected with Kali.
Lord, please cleanse us from all unrighteous roars, and restore Your righteous roar to me and my generational line.

Lord, I repent for all those in my generational line who were foolish and turned from God and invited or allowed Kali or death to be their shepherd, guiding them in this world as well as the spirit realm.
Lord, please pull me and my generational line out of any unrighteous depth or any other unrighteous place that Kali, death, or any other unrighteous spiritual being has been allowed to lead us into and trap us because we turned away from God.

I repent and renounce for all unrighteous breastfeeding.
I repent for all those who fed themselves off of the breasts of Kali, instead of feeding off of El-Shaddai. ~ 1 ~
Lord, please break off of me and my generational line the

consequences that came from feeding off of Kali, instead of feeding off of You, Lord.

I repent for all those who got their power, strength, and energy from Kali.
Lord, I declare that You and You alone are the Way, the Truth, and the Life.
Lord, You are my source of life, strength, and energy.

I repent and renounce for all those in my generational line who revered and worshiped the Hindu god Shiva as the supreme god, the destroyer, the standard of invincibility, might and terror; the ravisher, the transformer, the lord of the dance, the pure one, the one who purifies everyone by the very utterance of his name, the one who can never have any contamination, the god of the roaring storm, the one who can kill the forces of darkness, the wild one, the fierce god, the one who captivates, the teacher of yoga, music and wisdom; the one who conquered death, the one who is a pillar of flame, and any other attributes or titles of Shiva.
I renounce the Hindu god Shiva in all his forms, and depictions and all his attributes and titles.
Lord, please disconnect me and my generational line from Shiva and all his attributes and titles.

I repent for all those who worshiped Shiva as the on who conquered death, instead of worshipping the only one with the power to truly vanquish death; Jesus Christ, who with His death and resurrection destroyed death once and for all.

I repent and renounce for all those in my generational line who revered and worshiped the manifestations of Shiva in the five elemental substances; water, fire, air, earth, and ether.

I renounce all unrighteous fertility, unrighteous fierceness, unrighteous violence, unrighteous fearlessness, and unrighteous warfare connected with Shiva.
I renounce all lust, sexual immorality, and adultery connected with Shiva.

I renounce Shiva and Nandin the bull he rides on.
I renounce any and all jewelry and tokens that Shiva wears or carries around with him, including the ornament of serpents, the skull necklace, the garland of snakes, the trident, the drum-shaped hourglass, and any other pieces of jewelry or tokens connected with Shiva.

I repent for and I renounce all mantras chanted to Kali, Shiva, or any other Hindu gods or goddesses. ~ 2 ~

I repent for all those in my generational line who used or created unrighteous words and unrighteous sounds in worship, especially to Kali and Shiva.
I repent for all those who used unrighteous music to allure or seduce people.
I repent for and I renounce all use of the Aum sound. ~ 3 ~
Lord, please disconnect me and my generational line from any unrighteous worship, words, sounds, rhythms, vibrations, or lights, and cleanse me and my generational line from all of these substances.
Lord, please restore Your glory sound to me and my generational line.

I repent and renounce for all those in my generational line who used or worshiped the five unrighteous senses and the five organs of perception of Shiva.
Lord, I repent for all those in my generational line who used their five senses and their gift of discernment for evil.
Lord, please break the consequences of this wickedness off

of me and my generational line.
Lord, please come and cleanse me and my generational lines five senses and our gift of discernment from any and all defilement that came from these sins.

I repent and renounce all meditation and yoga connected to Kali or Shiva.

Lord, please come and unseat and remove Kali and Shiva from between me and my spouse, from any place in our physical or spiritual wombs, and any other place that they have been allowed to be.
Lord, please come and cleanse every part of our beings that have been defiled by these unrighteous beings.

Lord, I ask that You would come and remove any and all gods and goddess off of us, as well as any substances or spirits that they brought with them.
In the Name of the Lord Jesus Christ, I command Kali and Shiva to leave me, my physical and spiritual womb, and any other place that they have been allowed to be. You are no longer welcome her, go and take all that pertains to you with you.

Lord, please come and replace them with the righteous being that You intended to be between, or around me and my spouse.
Lord, I invite You to come and take Your rightful place of authority over me and my spouse, our marriage, and over our family.
Lord, please bring me, my spouse, and every aspect of our marriage back into right alignment with You.

Lord, I ask that You would come and cleanse our physical and spiritual wombs from all defilement and death that came from Kali and Shiva.

Lord, please bring our physical and spiritual wombs back into correct alignment with You, back into Your righteous time.

Lord, please come and cleanse any and all defilement that came upon our physical and spiritual wombs, and defiled the embryo, the water in the womb, the umbilical cord, the zygote, or any other part of the womb.

Lord, please heal our wombs from all trauma, wounding, or scars.

Holy Spirit, I ask that You would come and inhabit the physical and spiritual wombs of this generational line.

Lord, please return anything that was stolen from us, by Kali Shiva, or any other unrighteous spiritual being.

Lord, I ask that You would cleanse our marriage and our love life from all defilement that came through Kali and Shiva.

Lord, I ask that You would restore our love life to the pure and holy ecstasy You intended it to be.

Lord, please remove any part of our marriage from any unrighteous place that Kali or Shiva was allowed to trap us.

Lord, I ask that You break, shatter, and destroy any unrighteous networks or any other unrighteous setups between me and my spouse that came from Kali and Shiva.

Lord, I ask that You would restore all the righteous spirit, soul, and body ties and connections and any other righteous ties or connections that You intended to be between me and my spouse.

Lord, please cleanse these righteous ties and connections from all defilement.

Lord, I ask that You would restore anything that the enemy

was allowed to steal from us.

Lord, I ask that You would cause our marriage to grow in purity, love, and intimacy.

1. ~~

Pronounced el shad-dy, it means "The All-Sufficient One" and is usually translated in English as "God Almighty".

~~ The Hebrew word "dai" means to {shed forth} or {pours out} which suggests provision and blessing. Thus, God is the All-Sufficient One

~~ The Hebrew word "shad" or "shaddayim" means breast or breasts and occurs 24 times as "Shaddai" and signifies One who nourishes, supplies, and satisfies. Combined with the word "El" it then becomes the One mighty to nourish, satisfy, and supply."

2. ~~

A mantra is supposedly a formation of words, an utterance, a chant or prayer that is seen as sacred in Hinduism, Buddhism, Jainism, and Sikhism. They are believed by those who practice them to carry supernatural and spiritual powers.

3. ~~

Aum is a sacred sound in Hindu religion, it is a mantra in a few religions as well. In Hinduism, it is one of the most strong and important spiritual symbols. It is a mantra, a spiritual incantation spoken during certain rituals.

Caleb Peterson

MARRIAGE PRAYER
Caleb Peterson

There isn't much of a backstory to this prayer. It came along not long after the prayer to remove Hindu gods and goddesses between couples. It was another prayer I wrote to help my friend's marriage, and other couples dealing with issues and problems in their marriages. As well as single people who are looking to get married, who may have marital junk in their generational line.

Prayers for Generational Freedom

~ PRAYER ~
MARRIAGE PRAYER

I repent and renounce for all those in my generational line who cursed married people or marriage itself.

I repent and renounce for all those in my generational line who forced their children into unrighteous marriages, in order to gain money, status, or honor.

I repent and renounce for all those who sold their children or their wives to people of high status and wealth; for financial gain, or because of pressure or fear.

I repent for all those in my generational line who in order to gain status and favor, pressured their daughters to lay with men in high standing even when the men were married, for the purpose of producing a male heir because their current wife was unable to do so, or was only bringing forth girls.

I repent and renounce for all those in my generational line who prostituted their sons, daughters or wives for financial gain.

I repent for all those who sold their wives, their daughters, or their sons into the sex trade.

I repent for all those in my generational line who gave their wives or daughters to their debtors in order to pay an outstanding debt.

I repent for all those who took men's wives or children as payment of a debt that could not be paid.

I repent for all those who bet their wives or their daughters in any gambling events and lost them to other men.

I repent for all those who allowed other men to rape or commit sexual acts with their wives or daughters, while they stood by and watched.

I repent for all those in my generational line who mutilated, tortured and tormented, sexually abused or raped women while making their husbands watch or the other way around.

I repent for all those who mutilated, tortured and tormented or brutally murdered men or women while making their spouses watch.

I repent for any men in my generational line who killed husbands so that they could have their wives.
I repent for all those who murdered their spouse out of hatred or anger, or because they wanted to be with someone else.

I repent for and I renounce for all those in my generational line who believed and practiced Droit d'Seigneur or ius primae noctis, a practice that enabled the owners of feudal estates to deflower virgins on their wedding night to other men.
I repent for and I renounce for the practice of bringing all women about to become brides before the King that he may lay with them.
I repent for and I renounce any and all religions or cultures that practiced the deflowering of virgin brides on their wedding night by Kings, Chiefs, or men of high reputation, or wealth.
Lord, please break the consequences of these sins off of me and my generational line.

I repent for and I renounce any and all religions or cultures

that practiced or encouraged Polygamy, the practice of a male or female having more than one spouse.
I repent for all those who married family members, and for all those who forced relations to marry each other.
I repent for and I totally renounce for all generational incest.

I repent and renounce for all those in my generational line who dedicated or sacrificed virgin brides to any unrighteous spiritual beings on their wedding night.
I repent for all those who made virgin brides commit sexual acts with any human being, any animals, or with any unrighteous spiritual beings on their wedding night.

I repent and renounce for all unrighteous union with any human beings, stars, planets, any other heavenly bodies, any other gods, or any other unrighteous spiritual beings.
I repent for all those in my generational line who came into unrighteous union or committed adultery with any evil spirits, familiar spirits, incubus and succubus spirits, or any other unrighteous spiritual beings.
I repent for all those who had night husbands, {spirit husbands} and night wives {spirit wives}.
I repent for the breaking up of marriages, covenants, oaths, vows, divorces, and the destroyed relationships that have resulted from having relations with these spirits.

I repent and renounce for all those who practiced rape, assault, sexual abuse, and sadism in their marriage.
I repent and renounce for all those in my generational line who practiced any and all forms of unrighteous beauty, unrighteous nakedness, unrighteous seduction, and unrighteous allurement in their marriage.
Lord, I ask that You would cleanse me and my generational line's blood and DNA, from any and all defilement that came

upon us because of our sins.
Lord, please break the consequences of these sins off of me and my generational line.

I repent for all those in my generational line who sacrificed their spouse to the sun, the moon, the stars, the planets, any other heavenly bodies, any other gods, or unrighteous spiritual beings.

I repent and renounce for all those in my generational line who sacrificed married couples in any unrighteous rituals.

I repent for all those who married any animals or any unrighteous spiritual beings in any unrighteous wedding ceremonies.
I repent for all those who invited or allowed any unrighteous priest or priestesses, any other gods, or any other unrighteous spiritual beings to officiate their wedding ceremony.
I repent and renounce for all those in my generational line who performed or participated in any occultic wedding ceremonies.
I repent and renounce for all those in my generational line who performed their wedding ceremony in any unrighteous heavenly place, in any unrighteous dimension or realm, or in any place in the unrighteous depth, or the unrighteous deep.
I repent for all those in my generational line who consummated their marriage in any unrighteous dimension or place.
Lord, please remove me, my spouse, and any part of our generational lines that are trapped in any unrighteous place, please bring all these parts back to us and integrate them back where they are supposed to be.
Lord, please cleanse all parts that You are bringing back.

Lord, please cleanse me, my spouse, our marriage and both of our generational lines from all defilement that has come upon us through our sins.

Lord, I ask that You would come and break all unrighteous betrothals and marriages that my ancestors made.

Lord, please take off of me and my generational line any unrighteous engagement ring or wedding band, that was put on us through these unrighteous betrothals or marriages.
Lord, please break, shatter, and destroy all ties and connections that came upon us through these unrighteous unions, betrothals, engagements, or marriages.
Lord, I repent for coming into union with anyone or anything You did not intend us to.
Lord, please disconnect me and my generational line from any human being or any unrighteous spiritual being that we have come into unrighteous union with.
Lord, please bring back to me and my generational line any and all parts of us that were stolen or given away through these unrighteous unions. Please cleanse all these parts in Your blood, and please remove anything that the enemy was allowed to implant into us through these unrighteous unions.
Lord, please break the consequences of the sin of coming into unrighteous union off of me and my generational line.

I repent and renounce for all those who because of jealousy and envy cursed married couples.
I repent for all those who used witchcraft, sorcery, wizardry, black magic, voodoo, or any other unrighteous power to attack married couples and their marriage.

I repent for all those in my generational line who through evil practices trapped married couples in any unrighteous heavenly places or any place in the unrighteous depth.

I repent for all those in my generational line who knowingly or unknowingly separated and tore apart married couples.
I repent for all those who used any occultic power to separate married couples and therefore came under a curse by breaking up what God had placed together.
Lord, please forgives us, and remove any and all curses that came upon us, by breaking up what You had placed together.

I repent for all those in my generational line who twisted the original intent of the submission of women in marriage and dishonored the knowledge that women are co-heirs with Christ.
I repent for all the men in my generational line who used their authority as the head of the household to humiliate, abuse, and control their wives.

I repent on behalf of myself and my generational line for all the men who abdicated their responsibility for spiritual and physical leadership and authority and allowed their wives to step into the role as the head.
I repent for all the husbands in my generational line who did not extend their spiritual and physical headship over their wives.
I repent and renounce for myself and my generational line for the men who because of fear and passivity relinquished their responsibility as head.

I repent for all the women in my generational line who because of the lack of physical and spiritual leadership and headship, they stepped into and took over the position as head of the household.
I repent for all the women who would not allow their

husbands to step into the role as head of the household.
I repent for all the women who operated in control or a spirit of Jezebel, and emasculated the men in their lives. And took over the place of headship.

I repent and renounce for all those in my generational line who performed or participated in any same-sex wedding ceremonies.

I repent for and I renounce all generational same-sex marriages.
I repent and renounce for calling what You have called unholy, Holy; and what You have called Holy, unholy.
I repent and renounce on behalf of myself and my generational line for twisting Your Holy plan for marriage, for You made it to exist between a man and woman, and we twisted it and corrupted it.
Lord, please come and cleanse me and my generational lines blood and DNA from this evil, and any defilement that came through these sins.
Lord, I ask that You would cleanse and restore marriage in my generational line back to the Holy thing You created it to be. Please cleanse it from all contamination from the enemy.
Lord, please restore to me and my generational line the Holy Sanctity of Marriage.
Lord, I ask that You would place in me and my generational line a Holy respect, honor, and reverence for marriage the way You created it.

Lord, I ask that You would cleanse the marriages in my generational line from any and all contamination that came through any unrighteous unions, or through our sins.
Lord, I ask that You would restore my marriage and love life to the pure and holy ecstasy You intended it to be.
Lord, I ask that You would break, shatter, and destroy any

unrighteous networks, any unrighteous ties, and connections, or any other unrighteous setups between me and my spouse.

Lord, I ask that You would restore all the righteous spirit, soul, and body ties and connections, and any other righteous connections that You intended to be between me and my spouse, that the enemy was able to break or sever.

Lord, please cleanse these righteousness ties and connections from any and all defilement.
Lord, I ask that You would cleanse me, my spouse, and every aspect of our marriage in Your blood.

Lord, I ask that You would cleanse me and my generational line from all defilement that came through all of these sins and I ask that You would restore unto me and my generational line all innocence and purity that You implanted within us.

REPENTANCE OF STANDING IN DEFIANCE OF THE LAWS OF GOD

Caleb Peterson

This prayer started with a vision I guess you would call it. I was sitting in my room praying about some things that were happening in our nation. The fact that a lot of Christians are not only supporting sin but in ways, they are celebrating it. I was praying when this very vivid picture popped into my head. I saw the sky open up, and in the clouds was Jesus as the Lion of Judah. I could see a very hot fire burning in His eyes. Anger radiated from this fire. I got the sense he was extremely angry at His children. For they were in defiance of His very laws. He was coming to judge these sins, and His children were standing in the way.

He told me He was coming to judge these sins no matter what. And if His children stood in the way, then they would be receiving part of that judgment.

This was very frightening in a way. For I look around at the current state that the church is in and it's not good. Lots of pastors are supporting and celebrating sin, as well as teaching their congregation to do the same. And the members of these churches aren't questioning their pastors at all. They just go along with it, blindly following the blind. We have churches and ministries not only supporting absolute sin but going as far as to honor and celebrate it. Churches are supporting, celebrating and funding organizations that operate outside of God's law, that operate in wickedness. It has gotten to where Christians are either so blind to the truth that they can't see right from wrong, or they are too scared to go against the grain. We as the church have traded the Fear of the Lord, in exchange for the fear of man.

     We as the church need to repent and turn back to God. We need to throw off the fear of man and once again cloak ourselves in the Fear of the Lord. We need to call out for wisdom and discernment so that we can once again know good from evil. At this point, most Christians can't tell the difference between heaven and hell. To be able to survive the days to come we must walk in wisdom and discernment.

     We need to ask God's forgiveness for any time that we have stood in direct defiance of His holy laws, and any time that we supported, celebrated, or honored sin in any way. Like a lot of my prayers, this one started out as a personal prayer of repentance on my own behalf.

~ PRAYER ~
REPENTANCE OF STANDING IN DEFIANCE OF THE LAWS OF GOD

I repent on behalf of myself and my generational line for coming against, mocking, or defying God's Holy Laws.

I repent and renounce for all those in my generational line who came into agreement with and supported things that were clearly marked as sin in scripture, and therefore came into direct defiance of God's Holy Laws.

I repent for all those who came under a spirit of deception and believed lies and falsehoods, and supported sin in any way.
I renounce and repent for all those who not only supported sin but even went as far as to honor and celebrate it, as well as those who practiced these sins.

I repent for all those who through their wickedness or their support of wickedness, incurred the divine penalties for their actions and were cast into the hands of the living God. ~ 1 ~

I repent for all those who mocked the Word of God which says that the wages of sin are death, and not only continued in their sin, but also encouraged others in their sin.
I repent and renounce for all those who loved the wages of sin and unrighteousness. ~ 2 ~

I renounce and repent for all those in my generational line who loved wickedness and hated holiness and pureness of heart.

I repent for all those who loved what God hates, and hated what He loves.

I repent for all those who came against God's divine plan of holy marriage, and exchanged His truth for a lie.
I repent for all those who gave themselves over to uncleanness and to unnatural lusts and desires.
I repent for the Christians in my generational line who not only supported these sins but also participated in them as well and believed that God supported them.
I repent for all those who believed that these sins would go without punishment.

I repent for all those who were in unrighteous relationships and unions.
I repent for all the Christians who not only supported these unrighteous relationships and unions but believed that God supported them and was in them.
I repent for all those who were governed by or operated under a spirit of false love, instead of the Spirit and Being of Love who is; Jesus Christ.
I repent for all those who were deceived into thinking that this false love was God's love.
I repent for all those who supported and celebrated this false love.
I repent for all those who called this false love real true love.

I repent for all those who excused sin in the name of being loving, instead of taking a stand of purity and coming in love through holy correction.
I repent for all those who would not speak out against sin, who would not stand up for the truth and what was right. For they were either operating in the fear of man, or they were swayed by the rushing tide of our corrupt culture. The

culture that is ruled by deception, wickedness, and political correctness.

Lord, please forgive us for not standing up against the norm and speaking Your truth in boldness and love.

Forgive us for allowing fear and political correctness to sway us and cause us to do and say things that contradicted Your Word.

I repent for all those who supported, honored, or celebrated sin, for by doing so we brought upon ourselves the iniquity and the consequences that come with the very sin we supported.

I repent for all those who supported and celebrated sin and therefore positioned themselves between God and the people in sin. Therefore, they were in defiance of Him and His laws and stood between God and the very sin that He came to judge.

Lord, I repent on behalf and myself and my generational line for any time we stood between You and the sin that You came to judge.

Lord, please forgive us for standing in the way of Your judgment.

Lord, I ask that You would remove all judgment that came upon us for standing in defiance of Your laws by supporting and celebrating sin, and for standing between You and the very sin that You came to judge.

Lord, please cleanse us from the consequences of the sin of supporting, honoring, and celebrating wickedness.

1. ~ ~
Hebrews 10:31
31 It is a fearful and terrifying thing to fall into the hands of the living God {incurring His judgment and wrath}. ~ **Amplified Bible** ~
2. ~ ~
Romans 6:23
23 For the wages of sin is death, but the gift of God is eternal life in Christ Jesus our Lord. ~ **NKJV** ~

Prayers for Generational Freedom

THE TRUTH OF GOD
Caleb Peterson

This prayer does not have a whole lot of back story. I remember watching the posts of Christians on Facebook, and I was amazed at the level of deception on a lot of them. How they all believed such lies and falsehoods. How they would trade the truth for a lie. How they just believed every word coming out of the media's mouth. Why do we seem to believe anything as long as it's on the eleven o'clock news?

And there are of course others aspects to this. I am beginning to see more and more churches preaching things that do not line up with the Word of God, or the Spirit of Truth. We are beginning to see it more and more as more churches and more leaders are trading the truth for lies.
This isn't just happening in the church, we are starting to see a greater and greater level of lies and deception within our Government and our culture. I am shocked at the level of lies and deception that people are not only living in but calling the truth.

Scripture actually tells us to buy the truth and never sell it, unfortunately, I don't see the church doing that. I don't see people paying the price it takes in order to buy the truth and then hold it dear never selling it for it is beyond price. That is where this prayer came from, repenting for myself first of course.

Caleb Peterson

~ PRAYER ~
THE TRUTH OF GOD

I repent and renounce for all those in my generational line who suppressed, repressed, or hindered the Truth of God.

I repent for all those who camped in places of resignation and denial. Instead of actively seeking out the Truth of God in order to walk into deeper and deeper levels of freedom and purity.

I repent for all those who did not actively seek out the truth, but instead, they chose to live in falsehoods and denial.
I repent for all those who came into alignment with deceptions, lies, and falsehoods of the enemy.

I repent for all those who allowed the enemy to keep them in unrighteous thought patterns, mindsets, attitudes, views, temperaments, and beliefs through denial and deception.

I repent for all those who did not revere, honor, and treasure the Truth of God.

I repent for all those who either bought the truth and then sold it, or did not buy it at all because they did not feel it was worth the price that it cost to attain it.
Lord, forgive us for either not seeing Your truth as worth the price, or after buying it we didn't fight violently to keep it, but instead, we sold it to the highest bidder.
I repent for all those who sold the truth for wealth, riches, power, or fame.

I repent for all those who traded the Truth of God for a lie.

I repent for all those who valued lies, falsehoods, and deception above the truth.
I repent for all those who did not rise up against and attack the lies of the enemy, but instead embraced them.
I repent for all those who embraced the lies and deceptions of the enemy because they were easier to handle than embracing the truth.
I repent for all those who allowed lies, falsehoods, myths, and deceptions to enter in heart and then settle in and invade their being.

I repent for all those who instead of spreading and imparting truth, they spun webs of lies and proclaimed and dispersed deceit.

I repent for all those who did not bind mercy and truth around their necks and did not write them on the tablets of their hearts. ~ 2 ~

I repent for all those who did not allow the Truth of God to purge and cleanse all wickedness from their hearts, and all falsehoods from their mind, will, and emotions.

I repent for all those who hated the truth and would not allow it to be spoken around them.
I repent for all those who would only allow friends around them who would tickle their ears with fiction instead of the sometimes painful truth.
I repent for all those who would rather embrace the kisses of their enemies than the wounds of their friends. ~ 3 ~

I repent for all those who utterly refused sound doctrine and teaching, as well as wisdom and truth.
I repent for all those who turned their physical and spiritual ears away from the truth and turned to falsehoods, lies, and

fables.

I repent for all those who refused to be challenged with and by the truth.

I repent for all those who would not allow any form of truth to come around them, they removed friends and family from their midst who sought out and spoke the truth. And they brought into their midst advisors who only told them what they wanted to hear, and teachers and friends who would tickle their ears with fables that went down easy. People who would support the unrighteous mindsets that they held dear, who would support the fables they believed to be true. Someone who would tell them they were going in the right direction, when in fact, they were headed down a dark path. ~ 4 ~

I repent for all those who did not listen to or receive the Spirit of Truth when He came to them.

And when He had come they would not allow Him to guide and take them on a journey of discovering and uncovering all truth.

I repent for all those who would not be led by the Spirit of Truth and would not allow Him to tell them of things to come. ~ 5 ~

I repent for all those who rejected the truth, for in doing so we rejected the Lord of All; Jesus Christ. ~ 6 ~

I repent for all those in my generational line who not only would not receive a love of the truth but actively scorned and rejected it when it could have saved them.

And for that reason, God sent upon them strong delusion and deception that they would believe and follow lies and falsehoods, that all those might be condemned for they did not believe the truth but took pleasure in wickedness and unrighteousness. ~ 7 ~

Lord Jesus, I ask that You would come and remove all condemnation, defilement, as well as any and all curses that came upon us through these sins.

Lord, please forgive us for rejecting Your truth, and for not seeking it out, but instead choosing to live our lives in denial and deception.

Lord, I ask that You would cause us to react in a righteous way when the Spirit of Truth comes knocking at our door.

Cause us to fling the door wide open inviting Him into our lives.

Cause us to follow Him on a journey of seeking out and uncovering the truth wherever it has been hidden. Cause us to go on an amazing treasure hunt, seeking out the riches of the Truth of God.

I declare on behalf of myself and my generational line that we want and desire You to guide us into every fiber, and every aspect of the truth.

1. ~ ~
Proverbs 23:23
23 Buy truth, and do not sell it;
buy wisdom, instruction, and understanding. ~ **ESV** ~
2. ~ ~
Proverbs 3:3
3 Let not mercy and truth forsake you;
Bind them around your neck,
Write them on the tablet of your heart, ~ **NKJV** ~
3. ~ ~
Proverbs 27:6
6 Faithful are the wounds of a friend,
But the kisses of an enemy are deceitful. ~ **NKJV** ~
4. ~ ~
2 Timothy 4:3-4
3 For the time will come when people will not tolerate sound doctrine and accurate instruction {that challenges them with God's truth}; but wanting to have their ears tickled {with something pleasing}, they will accumulate for themselves {many} teachers {one after another, chosen} to satisfy their own desires and to support the errors the hold,
4 and will turn their ears away from the truth and will wander off into myths and man-made fictions {and will accept the unacceptable}.
~ **Amplified Bible** ~
5. ~ ~
John 16:13
13 However, when He, the Spirit of Truth, has come, He will guide you into all truth; for He will not speak on His own authority, but whatever He hears He will speak; and He will tell you things to come. ~ **NKJV** ~
6. ~ ~
John 14:6
6 Jesus said to him, "I am the way, the truth, and the life. No one comes to the Father except through Me. ~ **NKJV** ~
7. ~ ~
2 Thessalonians 2:10-12
10 and by unlimited seduction to evil and with all the deception of wickedness for those who are perishing, because they did not welcome the love of the truth {of the gospel} so as to be saved {they were spiritually blind, and rejected the truth that would have saved them}.
11 Because of this God will send upon them a misleading influence, {an activity of error and deception} so they will believe the lie,
12 in order that all may be judged and condemned who did not believe the truth {about their sin, and the need for salvation through Christ},

Prayers for Generational Freedom

but instead took pleasure in unrighteousness. ~ **Amplified Bible** ~

Caleb Peterson

REPENTANCE OF ALL SELFISH LOVE
Caleb Peterson

This prayer started out after a very hurtful breakup. The pain and heartache were all I could think of. But in the midst of all that, God brought someone to speak into my life. They showed me where at certain times I had been selfish in my love. It really threw me for a curve. So I sat in my room repenting of my selfish love, for asking my girlfriend to fill holes in my heart she couldn't fill. And repenting of not being selfless in my love towards her in every aspect. I realized at times I came to her so she could love on me not the other way around.

I started to pray about it coming before God asking His forgiveness for my selfish love. Then suddenly I felt an extreme sadness. I could feel a sorrow coming from the heart of Jesus. And then it hit me right between the eyes. This is exactly what a lot of Christians do to God. We come before Him when we need to feel love, or we need something. When do we come before Him just to give Him love, to just lavish Him with love? How often do we wake up in the morning and ask God what He needs from us today? When do we come before Him in the evening asking Him how His day went? When do we come before His throne just to lavish Him with our love?

Our God is the King of Kings, the Creator of the Universe, the Uncreated God. And this immense being of power needs and desires one thing; our love! How would you feel if the person you were dating or married to, only came to you to get love or affection not to give it? One sided relationships are not fun, especially for the person who is making all the effort. And yet no matter what, God is constantly opening up His heart to us and lavishing us with love. No matter how many times we come to Him just to receive love He never closes His heart to us, even if it really hurts that we don't come just to love on Him at times. No matter how many times we hurt Him, He always remains vulnerable to us.

We need to get to where at times we come to Him in worship and in love, expecting nothing in return. Where we come just to pour our love upon Him in total surrender. We need to wash His feet with our tears of joy, love, and affection.

This prayer came from this amazing revelation. As soon as God showed me His aching heart. I started repenting for being selfish in my love, especially in my love towards Him, and this prayer was born.

Caleb Peterson

~ PRAYER ~
REPENTANCE OF SELFISH LOVE

I repent and renounce on behalf of myself and my generational line for all selfish love and all false love.

I repent and renounce for all the times I was selfish in love, loving only when love was returned, or loving for the sole purpose of receiving love in return.
I repent for all those who loved only if and when love was given to them.
I repent on behalf of myself and my generational line for refusing to give affection and love unless it was in turn given back to us.

I repent for all those who were not selfless in love, for true love is not self-seeking.
I repent for all those who's express reason for giving love was to receive it.

I repent for all wrong and for all selfish motivations in love.

I repent for all those who threw love away when times got tough, instead of fighting in order that their love might grow and warring to keep love's flame alive.
I repent for all those who would not take the time and effort in order to build love into a strong, unshakable structure.
I repent for all those who quit in times of trouble, instead of warring for love and coming to the realization that anything worth having doesn't come without some sort of battle.
I repent for all those who believed that love was easy one hundred percent of the time, and when it got tough they gave up.

I repent for not putting in the time and effort to create and build love, for true love is built over time, true love is forged in fire, and must be fought for on a daily basis.
Lord, please forgive us for true love believes all things, hopes all things, and endures all things; real love remains steadfast during difficult times without waning or growing weary.

I repent for being selfish in love and expecting the people in my life to fill the void within my heart that only the love of God can fill, that only the affection of God can touch.
I repent for asking the people around me to fill and to touch the deep places of my heart that only God can touch and fill.
I repent for asking the people in my life to touch the deep places of my being that call out to the deep places of God, for deep calls out to deep.

I repent for allowing this world and the cultures therein to not only teach me about love but to dictate my feelings and mold my opinions of what true love should look like.
I repent for allowing Hollywood movies, actors, actresses, and musicians to shape my mindsets and views of what true love is.
I repent for coming into alignment with the idea that unrighteous acts done with someone you love constitutes true love.
I repent for allowing the enemy to use movies, music, or the media to shape my mindsets of what true love looks like.
I repent for turning to the world to see what true love should look like, instead of turning to the very essence and being of love, Jesus Christ.

I repent for not walking in true love, and loving those in my life even if they did not return that love.
I repent for not walking in Jesus' example of true love,

loving the people around us even if it was never returned, as well as laying down my life for my friends.
I repent for not being that pure example of love, mirroring God in all my ways.

I repent for anytime I was selfish in my love towards You, Heavenly Father.
I repent for being selfish in my love towards you God, and for only coming before You when I needed love or needed something else.
I repent for being selfish in my relationship with You God, and not returning the love that You continue to lavish upon me day after day.
I repent for any time when my relationship with You was one-sided and I only cared about getting my own needs and desires filled.

You are the God of the universe, the King of Kings, and yet even You need and desire love and affection.
You created me because You desired a lover.

I repent for not pouring my love on You like a fragrant offering.
I repent for taking and taking and not equally giving love in return.
I repent for living my life in duty, coming before You in obligation once a week, instead of coming before You in absolute delight and joy.

Lord, I ask that You would come and cause my heart to yearn and to ache for You.
Lord, please come and put Your hand into the lock of my heart, awakening my sleeping, darkened heart leaving my hands as well as my heart dripping with liquid myrrh, causing my heart to burn with a fervent burning flame of

love and zeal. Sending me on a journey of love. An adventure of seeking You out for the rest of my life.

Caleb Peterson

FAMINE OF THE TRUTH AND THE WORD OF GOD
Caleb Peterson

This prayer came forth from another friend asking me to write a prayer for them. She was either experiencing this first hand or seeing a friend go through it. She came to me with a verse and asked for a prayer about a famine of the word of God. I told her I would see what I could do.

As I began studying and praying about this issue, I started to see this issue a lot, especially in the church. I not only began to discern an extreme famine of the word of God within churches but also an underlying hatred for the Word of God in a lot of Christian circles. It feels like we want to go our own way, and do things our own way. We pretend to care about what the Will of God is, and yet we very rarely seek Him for advice in our daily lives. Whether it is in prayer or through His word. We don't want to hear the truth, whether it comes from a friend, God's voice, or from the word of God. We just want to hear things that tickle our ears and go along with the mindsets that we so vainly cling to.

It feels like we as the church are in a famine. A famine of the truth of God, as well as the word of God. Which is very sad, for we will not make it in the days to come if we are not rooted and grounded in the truth and word of God. We are being tossed to and fro, by every wave of doctrine that comes our way, not only that but we are ensnared and we follow the doctrines of our wicked culture.

~ PRAYER ~
FAMINE OF THE TRUTH AND THE WORD OF GOD

I repent for all those who turned to the right and to the left instead of walking a straight path after God. ~ **1** ~

I repent for all those who allowed to allowed the Book of the Law of God to depart from their heart as well as from their lips.
I repent for all those who did not meditate on it day and night or observe and follow that which was written. ~ **2** ~
Lord, please break off the curse of poverty, misfortune, and unrighteous sorrow that came upon us from these sins.

I repent for all those who did not rejoice and delight in the law of the Lord. ~ **3** ~

I repent for all those who demeaned the Word of God and the anointing and power it possesses.
I repent for all those who despised the Word of God and did not fear His commandments.
I repent for all those who hated or blasphemed against God, for in doing so not only did we blaspheme against the Lord Most High but against His word as well, for scripture tells us God is the living breathing Word. ~ **4** ~
Lord, please break the consequences of these sins off of me and my generational line.

I repent for all those who did not take the Word of God literal, word for word.
I repent for all those who denied the truth that resides in

and the truth that is the Word of God.
I repent for all those who attempted to twist or pervert the meaning of scripture in order to suit their own agendas.

I repent for all those who evaluated and placed their written traditions at the same level or above in stature and authority of the Word of God.
Lord, forgive us for placing our words or written traditions at the same level or higher than Your Holy Word.

I repent for all those who believed that their spiritual leaders were above the authority of the word of God, or that they could overturn or invalidate scripture.
I repent for all the leaders who taught this unrighteous doctrine, as well as believing it.

I repent for all sins that brought upon us the consequences of the Lord sending a famine of hearing the words of God.
Causing us to wander to and fro, staggering from sea to sea, seeking out the word of the Lord but never being able to find it.
Lord, please come and cleanse us from everything that keeps us from being able to find and hear Your word. Help us to be able to fill this divine hunger, this longing for Your words of life. ~ 5 ~

I repent for all those who utterly rejected wisdom, instruction, and knowledge.
I repent for all those who rejected and would not endure sound doctrine, or righteous wisdom and instruction, but would only listen to words of comfort, words of convenience, and words that tickled their ears. So they brought around the so-called advisors and friends who would only tell them what they wanted to hear. To speak to them words that would support the unrighteous mindsets

that they believed and held dear. Therefore their ears and hearts turned away from truth and they wandered off into myths, falsehoods, and man-made fictions. ~ **6** ~

I repent for all those who craved and placed more merit on myths and falsehoods than they did on the truth. For myths and falsehoods are easy to digest and the truth sometimes goes down hard and is hard to swallow.
I repent for all those who desired the kisses of their enemies rather than the wounds of a friend. ~ **7** ~
I repent for all those who would not listen to the truth if it was harsh, but would gladly listen to comforting lies.

I repent for all those who refused to hear the word of the Lord and attempted to pull people from the Path of Righteousness. ~ **8** ~

I repent for all those who would not give heed to the word of God.
I repent for all those who treated the word of God with contempt and reproach.
I repent for all those who did not rejoice and delight in the word of God.
Lord, forgive us for not giving heed to, rejecting, and not delighting in Your word.
I repent for all those who became so deceived and so hard of heart, that the Truth of God and the Word of God became an object of hatred and scorn for them.
Lord, I ask that You would come and unstop our ears, and remove all curses of deafness that came upon us because of these sins. ~ **9** ~

I repent for all those who attempted to live on bread alone and refused the life-giving word of God. For You said that man does not live by bread alone but by every word that proceeds from the mouth of God. ~ **10** ~

I repent for all those in my generational line who harbored an underlying hatred of the word of God.
Lord, please come and cleanse us spirit, soul, and body from all this hatred, as well as all defilement that it brought upon us.

Lord, please forgive us for not delighting in Your word, instead, we hated and despised it.
Lord, forgive us for all sins that we committed that brought about the consequences of a famine of the truth and the word of God being brought over our lives.

Lord, I ask that You would cause us to be open and ready to receive the truth, in any way that You deem necessary.
Lord, I ask that You would come and soften up the ground of our hearts, make us fertile and ready to receive the seed of Your word, and the water of Your truth.

1. ~ ~
Proverbs 4:27
27 Do not turn to the right or the left;
Remove your foot from evil. ~ **NKJV** ~

2. ~ ~
Joshua 1:8
8 This Book of the Law shall not depart from your mouth, but you shall meditate in it day and night, that you may observe to do according to all that is written in it. For then you will make your way prosperous, and then you will have good success. ~ **NKJV** ~

3. ~ ~
Psalms 1:2
2 But his delight is in the law of the Lord,
And in His law he meditates day and night. ~ **NKJV** ~

4. ~ ~
John 1:1
1 In the beginning {before all time} was the Word {Christ}, and the Word was with God, and the Word was God Himself.
~ Amplified Bible ~

5. ~ ~
Amos 8:11-12
11 "Behold, the days are coming," says the Lord God,
"When I will send hunger over the land,
Not hunger for bread or a thirst for water,
But rather {a hunger} for hearing the words of the Lord.
12 "People shall stagger from sea to sea {to the very ends of the earth}
And from the north even to the east;
They will roam here and there to seek the word of the Lord {longing for it as essential for life},
But they will not find it. ~ **Amplified Bible** ~

6. ~ ~
2 Timothy 4:3-4
3 For the time will come when the people will not tolerate sound doctrine and accurate instruction {that challenges them with God's truth}; but wanting to have their ears tickled {with something pleasing}, they will accumulate for themselves {many} teachers {one after another, chosen} to satisfy their own desires and to support the errors they hold,
4 and will turn their ears away from the truth and will wander off into myths and man-made fictions {and will accept the unacceptable}.
~ Amplified Bible ~

7. ~ ~

Proverbs 27:6
6 Faithful are the wounds of a friend {who corrects out of love and concern}, But the kisses of an enemy are deceitful {because they serve his hidden agenda}. ~ **Amplified Bible** ~

8. ~ ~

Isaiah 30:11
11 "Get out of the {true} way, turn aside from the path {of God},
Stop bothering us with the Holy One of Israel." ~ **Amplified Bible** ~

9. ~ ~

Jeremiah 6:10
10 To whom shall I {Jeremiah} speak and give warning, That they may hear? Behold, their ears are closed {absolutely deaf to God} And they cannot listen. Behold, the word of the Lord has become a reprimand and an object of scorn to them; They have no delight in it.
~ **Amplified Bible** ~

10. ~ ~

Matthew 4:4
4 But He answered and said, "It is written, 'Man shall not live by bread alone, but by every word that proceeds from the mouth of God.'"
~ **NKJV** ~

PROVERBS PRAYER
Caleb Peterson

This prayer basically came from studying my favorite book of the Bible. While studying Proverbs, I felt like I needed to repent for a lot of this stuff. It started off as a personal repentance and ended up being a written prayer. Hope it helps you as much as it did me.

Caleb Peterson

~ PRAYER ~
PROVERBS PRAYER

I repent for all those who were foolish and despised Wisdom, Knowledge, Understanding, and Instruction.

I repent for all those in my generational line who did not heed or refused to hear the instruction of their father, and for all those who forsook the law of their mother.
I repent for all those who did not daily bind them upon their hearts, nor did they tie them around their necks.

I repent for all those who allowed sinners to entice them into wickedness.
I repent for all generational shedding of innocence blood.
I repent for all those who cast their lots in with the wicked.
I repent for all those who walked the paths of the wicked and did not keep their feet from walking evil routes.
I repent for all those who's feet ran to evil.
I repent for all those who made haste to shed blood.
Lord, I ask that You would remove all unrighteous traps and nets off of me and my generational line, and bring back all life that was taken from us because of our sins.

I repent for all those who let perverse language issue from their lips.
I repent for all those who left the paths of uprightness, and chose to walk in the ways of darkness.
I repent for all those who rejoiced in doing evil, and took absolute delight in the perversity of the wicked.
I repent for all those who's ways were crooked, and all those who were devious in their paths.

I repent for all generational adultery, sexual perversion, and sexual immorality.
I repent for all those who followed the paths that lead to the house of the immoral woman.
I repent for all those who traveled the path that leads to death and the place of the dead.
Lord, cause us to stay on the paths of righteousness, and help us to walk in the way of goodness.
Lord, cause us to stay upright and blameless in all our ways.
Lord, I ask that You would remove all arrows that have been shot into our physical and spiritual livers because of our sexual sins, and cleanse us from any and all defilement and curses that came from these unrighteous arrows.
Lord, please come and remove any part of my being that is trapped or stuck in the house of the immoral woman, and the unrighteous dimension in which it resides.
Please cleanse these now freed parts from all defilement and disconnect me from these evil places.

I repent for all the women in my generational line who allured and seduced men into unrighteousness, especially married men.

I repent for all those who forgot the laws of the Lord, or refused to follow them.
I repent for all those who did not keep and treasure the commands of the Lord, and for all those who did not bind them on their finger and write them on the tablet of their hearts.

I repent for all those who did not bind mercy and truth around their necks, nor did they write them on the tablets of their hearts.
I repent for all those who instead of trusting God with all their heart, they leaned upon their own earthly knowledge

and understanding.
I repent for all those who did not acknowledge God in all their ways that He might direct their paths.
I repent for all those who were wise in their own eyes.
I repent for all those who did not fear the Lord and refused to depart from evil.
I repent for all those who walked and operated in the fear of man, instead of walking and operating in the Fear of the Lord.
I repent for all those who traded the Fear of the Lord for the fear of man.

I repent for all those who did not honor the Lord with their first possessions, and with the first fruits of all their increase.
I repent for all those who were stingy and hoarded their wealth, and in doing so robbed God of what was rightful His.

I repent for all those who rejected the might of the bull, the strength of the ox because it came in a undomesticated box and made a mess. They wanted everything clean and in order and so they rejected the ox and all the gifting and anointing it brings.

I repent for all those who rejected and utterly despised the correction and chastisement of the Lord.
I repent for all those who were totally devoid of understanding.
I repent for all those who refused and rejected the correction of their parents or of God.

I repent for all those who did not keep sound wisdom and discretion.
I repent for all those who allowed fear, terror, and horror to come over them as they slept.

I repent for all those who withheld good from those around them when it was in their power to help.
I repent for all those who devised evil against their neighbor.
I repent for all those who operated in jealousy and envied those who stood in the role of the oppressor.
I repent for all those who entered the paths of the wicked and walked the way of evil.
I repent for all those who lead their household into wickedness and brought upon themselves the curse of the Lord.
I repent for all those who were fools and operated in folly, and inherited a legacy of shame.

I repent for all those who partook from the table of evil, and ate the bread of wickedness and were intoxicated on the wine of violence.

I repent for all those who did not give attention to the words of God or incline their ear to His sayings.
I repent for all those who allowed them to depart from their eyes, and did not keep them in the midst of their heart.

I repent for all those who did not guard, protect, and keep their hearts with all due diligence.
I repent for all those who lived life with a deceitful mouth, and did not put perverse lips far from them.
I repent for all those who were foolish and therefore were snared and trapped by the words of their mouth.
I repent for all those who operated with a depraved tongue and allowed perversity to dwell in their hearts.
I repent for all those who through their words or actions sowed and spread strife and discord.
I repent for all those who allowed slander to issue from their lips, and for all those who purposely spread slander and

gossip.
I repent for all those who did not guard their mouths and restrain their lips.
I repent for all those who used harsh words in order to stir up anger and hatred.
I repent for all those who did not delight in and love purity of heart, and walk with grace and holiness on their lips, therefore we were not friends of the King.
Lord, I ask that You would remove all unrighteousness from our lips and mouths, that came upon us because of these sins.

I repent for all those who did not ponder the path of their feet.
I repent for all those who did not allow all their ways to be established by God so they might walk in righteousness in all their paths.
I repent for all those who did not remove their feet from evil.

I repent for all those who hated instruction, and despised correction.
I repent for all those who would not listen to or obey the voice of their instructors.

I repent for all generational adultery.
I repent for all those who drank water from cisterns that were not their own, and running water from other's wells.
I repent for all those who dispersed their personal fountains abroad, and allowed their streams of water to flow openly in the city streets.
I repent for all those who did not rejoice in the wife of their youth, and were not enraptured with her love.
I repent for all those who sought the love of others, therefore they were enraptured and ensnared by

immorality.

I repent for all generational laziness, especially such that lead to poverty.

I repent on behalf of myself and my generational line for operating in things that You Lord hate, including:
~ A prideful look
~ A lying tongue
~ Hands that shed innocent blood
~ A heart that devises wicked plans
~ Feet that are swift in running to evil
~ A false witness who speaks lies
~ And one who sows discord among his brothers.

I repent for all generational pride and arrogance.
I repent for all pride which led to us being chained in shame.
I repent for all those in my generational line who walked in and operated in foolishness.
I repent for all those who were proud of heart.
Lord, please remove the rod of pride from our mouths and cause us to walk in and operate in wisdom and discernment.

I repent for all those who did not use wisdom in choosing their friends, and discernment in choosing their fellowship.
I repent for all those who allowed unrighteous companions into their midst.
I repent for all those who hung around in the company of fools.

I repent for all generational hypocrisy.

I repent for all generational gossip.
I repent for all those who revealed secrets that were not meant to be spoken of.

I repent for all those who housed a perverse heart within themselves.

I repent for all the women in my generational line who lacked discretion and caused shame.

I repent for all unrighteous hoarding.
I repent for all those who trusted in earthly riches.
I repent for all generational covetousness.
I repent for all those who were greedy for gain, and allowed the love of money to guide them.
I repent for all those who were not diligent with what the Lord had given them, and squandered the wealth He gifted unto them.

I repent for all those who from their heart proclaimed foolishness.
I repent for all those who were not diligent with what the Lord had given them.

I repent for all those who hated or despised the Holy Scripture, the very Word of God.

I repent for all those who withheld correction from their children, and for all those who spared the rod of chastisement.

I repent for all those who closed their ears and hearts to the cries of the poor.
I repent for all those who did not have mercy on the poor, or even went as far as mocking them and their poverty.
I repent for all those who actively oppressed the poor.

I repent for all those who fed off of foolishness.

I repent for all those who dug up evil, who reopened unrighteous wells, and reawaken evil that had been buried or asleep.
I repent for all those who enticed their neighbors to sin.
I repent for all those who used sexual practices to led others away from the paths of righteousness.

I repent for all generational unrighteous rebellion.

I repent for all those who justified the wicked and the acts they committed, as well as those who condemned the just and pure of heart.
I repent for all those who loved transgression and evildoing.
I repent for all those who exalted their gate, for in doing so they sought destruction because of their arrogant pride.

I repent for all those who had a deceitful heart and a perverse tongue.

I repent for all generational bribery.
I repent for all those who used currency to lead others into wickedness and unrighteousness.

I repent for all those who isolated themselves from wise counsel and raged against all righteous judgment.
I repent for all those who operated in the lone wolf mentality.

I repent for all those who hated, mistreated, or drove away their parents.

I repent for all those who provoked others to anger.
I repent for all those who said, "I will repay evil with evil."

I repent for all those who gained wealth by deceitful means.

I repent for all those who ate the bread of misers and desired and savored his delicacies.

I repent for all those who wandered from the way of understanding.
Lord, please remove us from the assembly of the dead and cleanse our entire being from all death and defilement that came from us being imprisoned in any place of destruction and demise.

I repent for all those who sowed iniquity, and for all those who believed they could escape the consequences of doing so.

I repent for all those who removed and uprooted the ancient physical and spiritual landmarks which their fathers had set in place.
Lord, I ask that You would remove all curses that came upon us from removing these righteous landmarks.

I repent for all those who were jealous of sinners and the life they lead.
I repent for all those who were envious of wicked and evil men.
I repent for all those who plotted to do evil and commit wickedness.
I repent for all those who exalted themselves in the presence of the King, and took it upon themselves to stand in the place of the great. Therefore they were brought down low and greatly humbled.

I repent for all those who did not give bread to their enemy when they were hungry or water for him to drink when he was thirsty.

I repent for all those who did not have rule over their own spirit.

I repent for all those who were foolish and continued in and returned to their folly, like a dog to his vomit.

I repent for all those who attempted to ensnare or the trap the innocent.
I repent for all those who dug a pit for others, and in turn ended up falling into the very pit they had dug to trap others.

I repent for all those who would not accept the wounds of a friend and yet gladly accepted the kisses of an enemy.
I repent for all those who brought around themselves friends who would only tell them what they wanted to hear.
I repent for all those who were not righteous in their friendships and who were not discerning in their advice. They only told their friends what they wanted to hear, not what they truly needed to hear. For they were afraid of wounding or offending them with the truth. So they kept silent unless they had something to say that wasn't going to offend or get their friends mad.

I repent for all those who covered and hid their sins, instead of bringing them out into the light and confessing them.
I repent for allowing our sins to grow and fester in the darkness, instead of bringing them out into the light.

I repent for all those who trusted their own hearts, and therefore became fools.

Lord, as I repent for the all these sins I ask that You would come and remove any and all unrighteous defilement from my spirit, soul, body, heart, mind, will, and emotions.

Caleb Peterson

Lord, please break the consequences of all these sins off of me and my generational line.

Prayers for Generational Freedom

RESCUE FROM NEVERLAND
Caleb Peterson

I know most of you are going to think I'm crazy, as you look over this prayer, but this is very real. As a kid, I used to love the Disney movie; Peter Pan. But something about Pan always seemed to bother me, I just didn't know what it was. Then years later, when I saw the Once Upon a Time version of Peter Pan. I finally understood why I didn't feel right about Pan. So I did a bit of research and found that was very accurate. Pan is a being that seeks to sow and implant doubt in the minds of young boys. Causing them to reject sonship and instead accept a false version of it. Which in essence is actually a spirit of slavery.

Now I experienced this first hand in my own life. I was in a session with Dr. Paul Cox, he was conducting it on me of course. During the session, we discovered that a part of me was broken off from my being. It was a young boy, and as we were praying about this. Dr. Cox heard the word, "Abandoned", and I heard the phrase "Lost Boy". Instantly my mind when to Peter Pan. So we prayed and I spoke to that part of me that felt abandoned and that felt he would never truly be accepted and loved. I told him that no matter what anyone else had done to him, God would always be there for him. Then the Lord had my father who was sitting in on the session, put the young boy back into my being. It was an amazing session and I received a lot of healing from it.

This is, of course, the enemies plan. To get us to reject Sonship and accept his false version of it. He uses our pain, the wounds of our past, the rejection we have experienced, and fear of future rejection to cause us to embrace his false love and acceptance.

Years later I finally got time to finish that season of Upon Upon a Time. In it, Peter Pan was the bad guy. He was a dark being who used deception to lure boys to Neverland, and give them a false sense of acceptance, love, and home. As I watched these episodes my mind went back to that session years before. And I realized just how important that session had been.

Years later I felt something dark and sinister trying to pull parts of me back to Neverland, as well as trying to get me to once again accept the title of a Lost Boy. So I started asking the Holy Spirit what it was and I heard, "Pan's Shadow".

Now Pan's Shadow is an entirely different entity, an evil entity that brings darkness, dark substance, and dark matter with him. He is able to travel and port between realms and dimensions as well as change his appearance at will. Transforming into almost any form he so desires. This entity comes in the dead of the night. He is a being of extreme darkness. Through prayer, I truly believe that I heard the Holy Spirit tell me that this being is Darkness itself. He is the being named Darkness.

Now, of course, I fought this dark being, for there was no way I was going to accept that role again. I am a Son of God, not a lost boy. So I knew that there were still some roots that needed to be pulled out. Some things that hadn't been dealt with in that session. So I started writing a prayer, and this is the result.

Prayers for Generational Freedom

~ PRAYER ~
RESCUE FROM NEVERLAND

I repent for and I totally renounce all generational rejection, neglect, and abandonment.
I repent for and I totally renounce all generational manipulation and control.
I repent for and I totally renounce all generational selfishness, self-centeredness, cockiness, and arrogance.

I repent for all those who never wanted to grow up, and made any unrighteous decrees, declarations, proclamations, or vows that they would never do so.
I repent for all those who made any deals with any unrighteous beings, in order to stay forever young or attain immortality.
I repent for all those who refused to grow in maturity and stayed childish in many areas. ~ 1 ~
I repent for all those who refused to take up any and all responsibility, and for all those who abandoned the righteous responsibilities that God placed in their lives.
I repent for all those who refused to step into adulthood when the time came to do so because they didn't want to leave the carefree, duty-free life of a child.
I repent on behalf of myself and my generational line for coming into alignment with any unrighteous being that taught us to live off of milk, instead of maturing and eating meat. ~ 2 ~

I repent for all those who sought immortality and unending youth from unrighteous sources, and for all those who performed or participated in any rituals to gain it.
I repent for all those who sought after the Fountain of Youth

in order to gain unending life.

I repent for all those who performed or participated in any unrighteous rituals of attempting to gain immortality.

I repent for all those who used starstuff, or any other substances in order to gain unending youth. ~ 3 ~

I repent for all those who soared into the heavens using unrighteous means, and used the same means to travel to other dimensions.

I repent for all those who used pixie dust, start dust, or other substances to fly or to travel to other dimensions.

I repent for all those who attempted to change, warp, stop or lockout time.

I repent for all those who performed or participated in any unrighteous rituals to stop or change time and space.

I repent for all those who attempted to control or manipulate time and space.

I repent for all those who felt abandoned by their parents so they sought acceptance from spiritual beings that they did not know were evil.

I repent for all those who stole children from their families and made the orphans.

I repent for all those who through manipulation, control, coercion, or force; caused kids to reject their parents.

I repent for all those who allowed or invited unrighteous beings or spirits into their house and into their rooms.

I repent for all those who allowed unrighteous beings to take them into different dimensions and realms.

I repent for coming into alignment with any unrighteous being that made us believe that everyone in our lives would abandon us, and caused us to run away from all we knew, as well as causing us to run away from all commitment and love.

I repent for all those who came into alignment with the lie of the enemy that children are nothing but a burden.

On behalf of myself and my generational line, I repent for believing the lie of the enemy that we were a burden to our parents and our family, and that they would be better off if we had never been born or were gone.

I repent for coming into alignment with or allowing any beings, spirits, or substances of deception to come over us.

I repent for all those in my generational line who allowed abandonment and rejection to cause them to receive a spirit of slavery, bondage, as well as an orphan spirit, instead of receiving the Spirit of Adoption, by which we cry Abba Father. ~ 4 ~

I repent for all those who allowed abandonment and rejection to push them away from our Father in Heaven.

I repent for all those who allowed abandonment and rejection to lead them down dark pathways.

I repent for all those who because they had been abandoned by their earthly parents they allowed unrighteous beings to persuade them that God would abandon them as well.

I repent for all those who because of the wounds of rejection they refused to be led or fathered by God who is the King of Kings and the Father of the fatherless, instead they chose to be led, fathered, and ruled by Peter Pan: the King of the Orphans.

I repent for all those who refused the Sonship give to them by God, and were deceived into accepting slavery because it came in the form of a gift that seemed good, but in fact was false acceptance.

I repent for all those who traded their birthright of Sonship,

for slavery.
I repent for all those who rejected or laid down the mantle of the firstborn, the amazing inheritance that Jesus gave us, and all the blessings that came with it.

I repent for and I renounce all belief in Pan, a Greek deity who plays pipes to nymphs and is part human and part goat.
I renounce all connection between this deity and Peter Pan.
I repent and renounce all music used to hypnotize, mesmerize, seduce, or allure.
I renounce all unrighteous music, especially all unrighteous music associated with Peter Pan.
Lord, please remove all unrighteous music, rhythm, sound, and vibrations over me and my generational line.

Lord, please remove any mimicry spirits off of me and my generational line. ~ 5 ~

I repent on behalf of myself and my generational line for any time that we took on the mantle and title of a Lost Boy.
I now completely renounce and reject the mantle and title of: A Lost Boy.
Lord, I repent on behalf of myself and my generational line for rejecting our position as Sons of God.
Lord, I ask that You would come and remove that unrighteous mantle and title from me. Cleanse me spirit, soul, and body from all defilement that came with it.
Lord, please remove all false mindsets, all deceptions, and all lies from my heart, mind, will, and emotions, as well as any other place they have taken up residence in.

Lord, please remove Peter Pan from anywhere on, around, or in my being, and remove all substances, spirits, or defilement that came with him.

Lord, I ask that You would remove his shadow from any part of my being as well, and cleanse me from all darkness, evil substance, dark matter, and defilement that came through his shadow.

Lord, please cleanse my shadow from any defilement that came from being connected or associated with Pan's shadow.

Lord, please disconnect me from the being of Darkness that is Pan's shadow, and any dark place that he was able to trap any part of my being in. And please break, shatter, and destroy all ropes, cords, chains or other devices that are being used to try and pull any part of my being back into Neverland or any other unrighteous dimensions.

Lord, please cleanse my spirit, soul, and body from all pixie dust, star dust, starstuff, or dark matter that came from our association with Peter Pan and Neverland.

Lord, please remove all desensitization of our hearts and emotions that came with him, and all spirits or substances that have made us oblivious to the feelings of others.

Lord, please come and remove any spirit or substance that wounded or tainted our hearts, and made us unable to be loved or to love others.

Lord, please remove all fear of rejection and abandonment, and I repent for allowing them to dictate our emotions and our actions.

In the Name of the Lord Jesus Christ, I want to speak to any part of me that has been hurt, wounded, and rejected by those closest to them.

I want to tell you that I love and accept you. You are a wonderful part of my being and I need you.

God has and will always be there for you, He is our Father and He never has nor will He ever leave. He is always with us.

Please forgive me for any time that I rejected you in any way because I did not think you were valuable or needed.

It is safe to come back. I want you and need you. I welcome you back to the place within my being that God called you to be.

Lord, I ask that You would come and embrace this wounded part of my being and show him or her that You can be trusted and that You will never reject or leave them.

Lord, I ask that You would remove any part of my being that has been imprisoned or that has taken up a dwelling place in Neverland, and I ask that You would bring them back to me and integrate them in my being where You intended them to be.

Bring them back to me cleansed in Your blood, and integrate them into my being in proper alignment.

Please heal them of all scars and wounds that came through rejection and not being wanted.

Lord, please bring all these parts of me back into the right time and space, and mature them to the age they are supposed to be.

Lord, I ask that You would bring my entire being into alignment with You and Your righteous timeline.

Lord, cause me to mature and grow in Your timing, and cause me to follow Your leading no matter what path it takes me on.

Prayers for Generational Freedom

1. ~ ~
1 Corinthians 13:11
11 When I was a child, I talked like a child, I thought like a child, I reasoned like a child; when I became a man, I did away with childish things. ~ **Amplified Bible** ~

2. ~ ~
Hebrews 5:13-14
13 For everyone who lives on milk is {doctrinally inexperienced and} unskilled in the word of righteousness, since he is a spiritual infant.
14 But solid food is for the {spiritual} mature, whose senses are trained by practice to distinguish between what is morally good and what is evil. ~ **Amplified Bible** ~

3. ~ ~
Starstuff: Is a magical substance that supposedly fell to earth and contributed to Pan's everlasting youth.

4. ~ ~
Romans 8:15
15 For you have not received a spirit of slavery leading again to fear {of God's judgment}, but you have received the Spirit of adoption as sons {the Spirit producing sonship} by which we {joyfully} cry, "Abba! Father!" ~ **Amplified Bible** ~

5. ~ ~
Peter Pan is very skilled in mimicry, able to copy and imitate others voices as well as certain sounds. He uses this to trick and deceive.

Caleb Peterson

WARRIOR PRAYER
Caleb Peterson

This prayer came from a particularly rough season in my life. A season in which I had many battles come at me, one after another. It felt like I was going through an obstacle course. After conquering one hurdle I would get a brief rest and then another would be right in front of me. This was an extremely rough bumpy time in my life. So much so that I wanted to give up. So during this season, God began teaching how to not only fight for myself even when I thought I couldn't take anymore, but also teaching me to call out to Him in order that He might come and fight on my behalf. Through this season he taught me several things about being a warrior and showed me places in my life where I had given up and thrown aside the mantle of a warrior.

During this time He showed me two ways that He came when we prayed for Him to come and fight on our behalf. One way is when we are wounded and can't go on, so He comes and fights to us, carries us from the battlefield to a place of healing and then He fights the rest of the battle for us. The other way He fights for us is coming and giving us the strength and will to continue on and finish the current battle. Both ways are needed and valuable. But many times we just want God to come and fight the battle for us. Which He will at times, but at times He wants us to learn to fight on even when we think we can't go on. He will, of course, be there to give us the will to go on and the strength to do so. But He wants us to fight on and learn to endure.

Lots of us have given up because it has been too hard. We have laid down the mantle of a warrior because it's too difficult. Because the battles in our life have been too long, too bloody, too hard and too tedious; we have given up. God showed me that I had done just that. So I began to repent for any time I did so, later on, I decided to write it down as a prayer for others as well.

Caleb Peterson

~ PRAYER ~
WARRIOR PRAYER

I repent on behalf of myself and all those in my generational line for any time we laid down the call of God on our lives to be a warrior of the King.

I repent on behalf of myself and my generational line for all those who allowed the pain in their life to cause them to shut down or throw away the mantle of a warrior, instead of embracing the pain and allowing it to mold them and teach them lessons God wanted them to learn.
I repent for all those who because of the pain of the wounds they had received during the battle of life, they laid down their swords and refused to fight anymore, which only resulted in the enemy beating them to their knees and keeping them there.
I repent for all those who allowed their pain and the struggles they went through to make them a victim, instead of allowing God to use those things to make them stronger, and mold them into a fierce warrior.

I repent for all those who didn't want anything unless it came easy and therefore were not willing to pay the price it took to gain mantles and rewards God had for them.
I repent for all those who were not willing to pay the price that it took to gain victory in their relationships, in their personal lives, and in their spiritual walk.
I repent for all those who refused to war, because it was too hard, too painful, too bloody, and it took too much time. They wanted the victory to come easy and instant, instead of realizing that God is a God of process and that the battle would train them and strengthen them for things to come.

I repent for all those who forgot who they were in God, and therefore they could not fight or war against all that came to challenge their position in Christ.
I repent for all those who allowed the enemy to lead them into self-doubt and did not believe in themselves.
I repent for all those who did not violently fight for what was theirs, and what God had set aside for them.
I repent for all those who did not violently war to attain their birthright and fight vehemently to enter into all that God had for them.
I repent for all those who did not take the kingdom of heaven by force, who instead of being zealous and grabbing hold of the kingdom, were passive and refused to war in order that they might enter in. ~ 1 ~

I repent for all those who listened to the lies of the enemy, who told them they weren't strong enough, or that they could not withstand the raging storm, instead of believing Your word that we can do all things through Him who strengthens us. ~ 2 ~

I repent for giving up, thinking that the battle was too bloody and that we could not defeat the giants in our life, instead of believing that God would fight for us and that He would never allow a battle to come our way that we couldn't handle. ~ 3 ~

I repent for any time we forgot that we fight not against flesh and blood, but against evil rulers, authorities, mighty powers, and evil spirits in heavenly places. ~ 4 ~

I repent for all those who went into battle without putting on the whole armor of God and therefore were left vulnerable to attack and were hit and wounded by the burning arrows of the evil one. ~ 5 ~

I repent for all those who did not allow God to train them to be a warrior.
I repent for all those who did not allow God to teach them balance in being a warrior, for a warrior cannot live on war alone, a warrior cannot operate in aggression alone.
I repent for all those who did not allow Him to teach them righteous aggression as well as mercy, righteous rage, and wrath as well as gentleness.

I repent for all those who did not invite or would not allow God to come and teach their hands to fight and their fingers to war. ~ 6 ~

I repent for all those who came into alignment with false ideas and views of mercy.
I repent for all those who were not vigilant in their fight and did not properly watch their flank, therefore because the enemy could not take them head on he took them down from the inside using false mercy.
I repent for giving mercy when we shouldn't have and thus allowed the enemy to sneak spies into our midst.
I repent for all those who killed the people they were supposed to spare and spared the people they were supposed to kill. ~ 7 ~

I repent for all those who the enemy could not stop, so he pressed them onward and they lost all sense of mercy, grace, and gentleness.
I repent for all those who allowed the enemy to push them too far, push them over the edge into unrighteous aggression, and through this we allowed blood lust to enter in and take over, causing us to do things we wouldn't do otherwise.
Lord, cause us to operate in righteous balance, for even the most violent of warriors must know when to show mercy

and kindness.
I repent for all those who were not rooted and grounded in God's perfect love and therefore fear was allowed to come in and plants its seeds.
I repent for all those who allowed fear to keep them from becoming the fierce warrior God created them to be.
I repent for all those who allowed fear to keep them from traveling the path they were meant to walk upon.
I repent for all those who ran away in fear, instead of standing between the enemy and those who needed protection.
I repent for all those who allowed the fear of man, and the opinions of others to dictate their thought patterns, views, mindsets, and their actions.

I repent for all those who allowed fear into their hearts, instead of growing in righteousness and embracing boldness and becoming as brave as a lion. ~ **8** ~

Lord, I ask that You would come and remove from me and my generational line all fear of man. Come and root and ground us in Your perfect love, and cleanse us of all fear and create within us a bold, courageous heart. Cause a great roar to arise in our hearts. A roar of boldness. A roar of freedom. The roar and battle cry of a warrior!

I repent for all those who allowed weakness to overtake them and allowed their strength to be stolen from them to where they could not stand and fight.
I repent for all those who fell into despair and in their hearts gave up.
I repent for all those who tried to be someone else, instead of standing apart from the crowd; a diverse, strange, and peculiar masterpiece of God.
I repent for all those who embraced the lone wolf mentality

and were not wise enough to know when to ask for help in their battle.
I repent for all those who did not surround themselves with a righteous counsel, and a righteous fellowship of warriors to help them along their path, but instead tried to go it alone.
I repent and renounce the belief that a real warrior should suffer in silence, not allowing others to see the pain they are in.

I repent for all those who traded passion and zeal for passivity.
I repent for all those who attempted to kill the passion and zeal in them, for in doing so they killed off a huge part of the warrior heart within them.

I repent for all those who chose to lay down a walk-on part in the battle, for a lead role in a rusty cage.

I repent for all those who fought battles they were not supposed to fight, and for all those who refused to fight battles they were supposed to.
I repent for all those who never learned how to let God come and fight on their behalf. And for all those who believed if they didn't do all the fighting themselves, they were weak.

I repent for all those who believed their strength came from themselves, instead of from God.
Lord, we declare that You are our strength.
We declare that the Joy of the Lord is our strength. ~ 9 ~

Lord, I ask that You would awaken the warrior within me. The warrior spirit that never says die, that never gives in, and never backs down. The spirit that when my body is screaming out to give in, it screams out, "Never"!

I declared that I was not brought forth on this earth in defeat, and failure has no part in me, victory and triumph flow in my veins.
I declare that I am not a failure, I am a warrior of the King.

I refuse to hang around or listen to unrighteous talk of, whining, sorrow, self-pity, complaining, or cowardice. Those thoughts are contagious like cancer and produce the like.

I was not put on this earth to live an average, normal life.
I am more than a conqueror, I am a warrior!
Death and failure are not my destiny.
I am a warrior, and I have been hand chosen by the King of Kings.

I am not ashamed of my wounds and my scars, for they are part of my testimony, they are proof of how God brought me through the rough times, and they are reminders of when the enemy tried to break me but failed.
I declare that I am a warrior, I wasn't born one, I was made one through pain and through trials. Through pain and suffering, through getting knocked down, but having the will and strength to get back up again and conquer that which brought me to my knees.

I am an amazing instrument of God.
I am a powerful weapon, that will be used of God.
I am a sword in the hand of the King, I am an arrow in the quiver of the Holy Hunter.

1. ~ ~
Matthew 11:12
12 And from the days of John the Baptist until the present time, the kingdom of heaven has endured violent assault, and violent men seize it by force {as a precious prize - a share in the heavenly kingdom is sought with most ardent zeal and intense exertion}.
~ AMPC ~

2. ~ ~
Philippians 4:13
13 I have strength for all things in Christ Who empowers me {I am ready for anything and equal to anything through Him Who infuses inner strength into me; I am self-sufficient in Christ's sufficiency}.
~ AMPC ~

3. ~ ~
1 Corinthians 10:13
13 No temptation has overtaken you except such as is common to man; but God is faithful, who will not allow you to be tempted beyond what you are able, but with the temptation will also make the way of escape, that you may be able to bear it. ~ **NKJV** ~

4. ~ ~
Ephesians 6:12
12 For we do not wrestle against flesh and blood, but against the rulers, against the authorities, against the cosmic powers over this present darkness, against the spiritual forces of evil in the heavenly places.
~ ESV ~

5. ~ ~
Ephesians 6:10-11
10 In conclusion, be strong in the Lord {be empowered through your union with Him}; draw your strength from Him {that strength which His boundless might provides}.
11 Put on God's whole armor {the armor of a heavy-armed soldier which God supplies}, that you may be able successfully to stand up against {all} the strategies and the deceits of the devil.
~ AMPC ~

6. ~ ~
Psalms 144:1
1 Blessed be the Lord, my rock, who trains my hands for war, and my fingers for battle; ~ **ESV** ~

7. ~ ~
Ezekiel 13:19b
19 .... killing people who should not die and giving {a guarantee of} life to those who should not live, ~ **Amplified Bible** ~

8. ~ ~
Proverbs 28:1
1 The wicked flee when no one pursues,
But the righteous are bold as a lion. ~ **NKJV** ~
9. ~ ~
Nehemiah 8:10
10b Do not sorrow, for the joy of the Lord is your strength." ~ **NKJV** ~

Caleb Peterson

RENUNCIATION OF ALL UNRIGHTEOUS, CONTROLLING, AND MANIPULATIVE WORDS AND PRAYERS

Caleb Peterson

This prayer started from having to deal with the attack of Christian witchcraft. I know what most of you are thinking. What is Christian Witchcraft? There's no such thing! Ah, but there is! Christian witchcraft is a controlling or manipulative prayer. In essence, it is any prayer that is spoken outside of the will of God.

I will give you an example. I remember it like it was yesterday. My family and I had stopped going to a small church in our area because we did not feel welcome, wanted, and we hadn't been treated very well. So we prayed and felt the Lord telling us to leave. So we did, and so we decided to stay out of the church and do our worshiping and fellowshipping with God at home. Then after several months went by, we decided to go back one Sunday. A decision that was not liked by every family member. We entered the building and sat down. We were then approached by an elderly lady that went there. She laughed and turned to us and said, "I knew God would get you! I've been praying that He'd get you back into our church." As soon as she said that a shiver went down my spine. I looked over and my brother was cringing too.

This is a prime example of Christian witchcraft, or a controlling, manipulative prayer. In her mind, she assumed it was God's will that we attend this church or any church at all. She never stopped to think that we weren't happy here, or that God might have us outside church as most see it. She never stopped to actually ask God what His will was.

We as Christians need to be very careful what we assume and what we pray. We assume we know what God's will is and then we pray just that. When often times that is not what God's will is, that is just what we want or what we feel is right. We need to be careful, our words have more power than we think. And we can't allow the enemy to use our words to hurt or lead others in the ways we think they should go. Now I'm sure this lady had a good heart and meant well, but she was not praying the will of God. A good way to have prayed for us would have been to ask that the will of God be done in our lives, no matter what that looked like.

We must also watch the words of our mouth, and ask God to bridle our tongues. For scripture is very clear on being careful on what words we allow to proceed from our lips. It tells us that no word is to proceed from our lips except that which brings grace and edification to the listeners. So if we are speaking words that tear down, or discourage, demoralize, or dishearten others we are in contradiction of God's word. He tells us that no word is to proceed from our mouth, but what will lift up and edify those around us. Wow! I'm not going to lie, that is a tough one. I am certainly not there yet, but I'm getting there slowly.

And of course, nor can we allow witchcraft in any form to issue from our lips. We cannot just assume that we know the Will of God and pray it over others lives. Just because it looks good, or we believe it is what is best for them. We need to be very careful what we pray and what words we let issue from our mouths. Not only can these words damage others, but they can also turn right around and damage us just as bad. We need to be careful for in our mouth is the power of life and death. No matter what comes out of our mouth, whether it be life or death, we will end up eating the fruit thereof.

Caleb Peterson

That is where this prayer was birthed. Like most of my prayers, this one started out as a prayer of personal repentance and evolved into a prayer for others as well.

~ PRAYER ~
RENUNCIATION OF ALL UNRIGHTEOUS, CONTROLLING, MANIPULATIVE, AND UNEDIFYING WORDS AND PRAYERS

I repent for and I renounce on behalf of myself and my generational line for all those who knowingly or unknowingly prayed or allowed unrighteous, controlling, and manipulative prayers to issue from their lips.
I repent for and I renounce all generational Christian witchcraft.

I repent for all those who attempted to bring their will about through prayer, even if it was not what the Lord intended to happen.
I repent for all those who prayed things they felt were good, but in fact did not line up with the Will or Word of God.

I repent for all those who knowingly or unknowingly tried to control the movements of others through prayer.
I repent for all those who attempted to cause people to go certain places, or do certain things through prayer, instead of just praying that God's will be done in their life.
I repent for all those who assumed they knew the will of God for another and therefore prayed it into their life without asking God first.
I repent for all those who used manipulative prayer to lead others in ways they believed they should go.

I repent for all those who prayed outside the Will of God.
I repent for all those who did not listen to the words of the Father and then decree and pray it forth.

I repent for all those who did not follow Jesus' example of only doing what He saw His Father doing, and only praying what He heard His Father pray. ~ 1 ~

I repent for all those who did not watch or guard the words of their mouths and allowed them to run unbridled, and for all those who did not allow God to guard their mouths and the doors of their lips. ~ 2 ~

I repent for all those who did not allow God to muzzle their mouths when needed.
I repent for all those who professed to be wise, pure, and righteous, but did not bridle their tongues, therefore they were not only in sin but in deception as well. ~ 3 ~

I repent for all those who were foolish and allowed their mouths to run wild, and for those who did not hold their peace and shut their lips. ~ 4 ~

I repent for all those who did not keep their tongues from pouring forth wickedness, and from speaking and imparting guile to those around them. ~ 5 ~

I repent for all those who used their tongues as bows, and their words like arrows damaging, scarring, and wounding people with lies and falsehoods.
I repent for all those who proceeded from evil to evil, wickedness to wickedness in their walk of life.
I repent for all those who did not know, understand, or acknowledge the Lord Most High. ~ 6 ~

I repent for all those who used their words to scar, maim, and wound people; rather than using them to heal.
I repent for all those who's words were like swords and who used them to wound and slice people to the core.

Lord, forgive us for operating in foolishness and wounding people with our words, instead of being wise in all that we said to bring healing and comfort to those around us. ~ 7 ~

I repent for all those who allowed their untamed tongues to steer the ships of their lives like rudders and lead them into seas and oceans that they were never meant to voyage into.
I repent for all those who allowed their wicked tongues to be the helmsman of the ship of their life.
I repent for all those who allowed their unbridled, untamed tongue to contaminate and defile their physical and spiritual bodies.
I repent for all those who did not allow or invite God to bridle their mouths, guide their words, and tame their tongue. For our tongues are evil and full of venom and only God can tame and cleanse them.
Lord, I ask that You would come and tame my ruthless tongue, come and cleanse my tongue from all evil, wickedness, and all venom and poison. ~ 8 ~
Lord, I ask that You would come and cleanse my spirit, soul, body, mind, will, emotions, as well as the rest of my being from all defilement that came through allowing our untamed tongues to spew forth venom.
Lord, please come with Your coal of burning fire and place it on my lips and tongue, cleansing them from all wickedness and impurity.
Lord, cause me to operate in righteousness and purity. Cause my tongue to speak forth truth, life, purity, and love. Cause my tongue to only speak the words that You God have called me to speak.

I repent for all those who did not realize the power that they possessed within their mouths and spewed forth unrighteous words, prayers, declarations, and decrees. Lord, please forgive us for not using our words to build up and to bring hope, strength, and life. For you said that within our mouth was the power of life and death. ~ **9** ~

I repent for all those who used their mouths, tongues, and lips for wickedness, using the same mouth that they bless people to also curse them as well. ~ **10** ~

I repent for all those who defiled and cursed their physical and spiritual bodies, their soul and spirit, or any other part of their being through the words of their mouth.
I repent for allowing profanity and words of filth to issue from our lips, as well as words of unbelief and doubt.
I repent for allowing any unrighteous and curseful words to come from our mouths. ~ **11** ~
Lord, please come and cleanse my entire being from any defilement that came upon me from the words of my mouth.

I repent for all those who were fools and spewed forth a multitude of words, instead of being wise and restraining their lips. ~ **12** ~

I repent on behalf of myself and my generational line for all the times that the thoughts of our hearts and the words of our mouths did not come into alignment with the Will of God, nor did they please Him. ~ **13** ~

Lord, please forgive us for not watching the words of our mouths, and for allowing our wicked hearts to remain unchecked.
Lord, forgive us for any time we assumed we knew what You wanted in a person's life and prayed it.
Lord, forgive us for any and all unrighteous, controlling, manipulative, or lifeless words and prayers.

1. ~ ~
John 5:19
19 The Jesus answered and said to them, "Most assuredly, I say to you, the Son can do nothing of Himself, but what He sees the Father do; for whatever He does, the Son also does in like manner. ~ **NKJV** ~

2. ~ ~
Psalms 141:3
3 Set a guard, O Lord, over my mouth;
Keep watch over the door of my lips. ~ **NKJV** ~
Proverbs 21:23
23 Whoever guards his mouth and tongue
Keeps his soul from troubles. ~ **NKJV** ~

3. ~ ~
James 1:26
26 If anyone thinks himself to be religious {scrupulously observant of the rituals of his faith}, and does not control his tongue but deludes his own heart, this person's religion is worthless {futile, barren}. ~ **Amplified Bible** ~

4. ~ ~
Proverbs 17:28
28 Even a {callous, arrogant} fool, when he keeps silent, is considered wise; When he closes his lips he is regarded as sensible {prudent, discreet} and a man of understanding. ~ **Amplified Bible** ~

5. ~ ~
Psalms 34:13
13 Keep thy tongue from evil,
and thy lips from speaking guile. ~ **KJV** ~

6. ~ ~
Jeremiah 9:3
3 They bend their tongue, {which is} their bow for the lies {they shoot}. And not according to faithfulness do they rule and become strong in the land; for they proceed from evil to evil, and they do not know and understand and acknowledge Me, says the Lord. ~ **AMPC** ~

7. ~ ~
Proverbs 12:18
18 There is one whose rash words are like swords thrusts,
but the tongue of the wise brings healing. ~ **ESV** ~

8. ~ ~
James 3:3-8
3 Now if we put bits into the horses' mouth to make them obey us, we guide their whole body as well.
4 And look at ships. Even though they are so large and are driven by

strong winds, they are still directed by a very small rudder wherever the impulse of the helmsman determines.
5 In the same sense, the tongue is a small part of the body, and yet it boasts of great things. See {by comparsion} how great a forest is set on fire by a small spark.
6 And the tongue is {in a sense} a fire, the very world of injustice and unrighteousness; the tongue is set among our members as that which contaminates the entire body, and sets on fire the course of our life {the cycle of man's existence}, and is itself set on fire by hell {Gehenna}.
7 For every species of beasts and birds, of reptiles and sea creatures, is tamed and has been tamed by the human race.
8 But no one can tame the human tongue; it is restless evil {undisciplined, unstable}, full of deadly poison. ~ **Amplified Bible** ~
9. ~ ~

Proverbs 18:21
21 Death and life are in the power of the tongue,
And those who love it will eat its fruit. ~ **NKJV** ~
10. ~ ~

James 3:10
10 Out of the same mouth come both blessing and cursing. These things, my brothers, should not be this way {for we have a moral obligation to speak in a manner that reflects our fear of God and profound respect for His precepts}. ~ **Amplified Bible** ~
11. ~ ~

Matthew 15:11
11 It is not what goes into the mouth that defiles a person, but what comes out of the mouth; this defiles a person." ~ **ESV** ~

Mark 7:15
15 There is nothing outside a person that by going into him can defile him, but the things that come out of a person are what defile him. ~ **ESV** ~

Mark 7:20-23
20 And He said, "Whatever comes from {the heart of} a man, that is what defiles and dishonors him.
21 For from within, {that is} out the heart of men, come base and malevolent thoughts and schemes, acts of sexual immorality, thefts, murders, adulteries,
22 acts of greed and covetousness, wickedness, deceit, unrestrained conduct, envy and jealousy, slander and profanity, arrogance and self-righteousness and foolishness {poor judgement}.
23 All these evil things {schemes and desires} come from within and defile and dishonor the man." ~ **Amplified Bible** ~

12. ~ ~
Proverbs 10:19
19 In the multitude of words sin is not lacking,
But he who restrains his lips is wise. ~ **NKJV** ~
13. ~ ~
Psalms 19:14
14 Let the words of my mouth and the meditation of my heart
Be acceptable in Your sight, O Lord, my strength and my Redeemer.
~ **NKJV** ~

ABOUT THE AUTHOR

Caleb is the creator and founder of Lions of War Ministries. Lions of War Ministries was founded with the main purpose of helping individuals find true freedom in every aspect of their life. Their mission and desire is to help free and liberate individuals, leaders, and ministries from the generational and other supernatural bondage holding them back. Caleb is a very capable prayer minister trained and commissioned through Aslan's Place Ministries. He is well educated in the gift of discernment and only proceeds in prayer as the Holy Spirit leads. Caleb operates in the gift of waiting on the Lord as to how he proceeds when writing prayers. His gifting and insight will bring much freedom to those who take advantage of the prayers in this manual.

www.ingramcontent.com/pod-product-compliance
Lightning Source LLC
Chambersburg PA
CBHW081454040426
42446CB00016B/3237